Buckland's
Dominö Divination

Fortune-Telling with Dominöes
and
the Games of Dominöes

Raymond Buckland

Buckland's Dömínö Dívínatïön

Fortune-Telling with Dominöes
and
the Games of Dominöes

Raymond Buckland

PENDRAIG
Los Angeles, CA 91040

Dömínö Dívínatíön
Fortune-Telling with Dominoes and the Games of Dominos
By Raymond Buckland
First Edition © 2010
by PENDRAIG Publishing

Cover Design &
Interior Typeset & Layout   Jo-Ann Byers Mierzwicki

PENDRAIG Publishing
Los Angeles, CA 91040
www.PendraigPublishing.com
Printed in the United States of America

ISBN: 978-0-9827263-1-0

Contents

Introduction

The History of Dömínöes

Dominoes are relatively new to Europe. Records indicate that they were first found in France and Italy in the 1700s. According to Joseph Strutt (*The Sports & Pastimes of the People of England, 1801*): "*Domino . . . (is) a very childish sport, imported from France a few years back.*" Toward the end of the eighteenth century they were introduced into England, probably by French prisoners. In China, dominoes are much more ancient, the first positive record of them there appearing in the twelfth century; though they were probably used there for divination, rather than for gaming. According to the Chu sz yam (*"Investigations on the Traditions of All Things"*) dominoes were invented in 1120 ce, by a man who presented them to Emperor Hui Tsung. However, there are accounts of domino use by a soldier named Hung Ming, who lived 181-234 ce.

On the Chinese dominoes, the dots apparently represent all the possible throws obtainable with two dice, so there are no blanks to be found on their tiles. In many parts of the Orient, the domino markings were also placed on playing cards, together with characters depicted from various folk stories or from history. According to Catherine Perry Hargrave (*A History of Playing Cards*, London: Houghton Mifflin, 1930) "*Long ago, dominoes were used for fortune-telling in China . . . but the ancient symbolism and traditions are lost.*" In this book I hope to help restore some of that symbolism and re-introduce dominoes as a viable system of divination.

Innuit Eskimos have their own version of dominoes, on which they gamble heavily! They use as many as 148 pieces; each piece with a large number of dots on it — there might be the equivalent of two double sixes, or 24 dots, on just one end of one tile. Dominoes are widely used in Korea and India even today.

The name *"domino"* is from the Latin dominus — *"Master of the House."* Divination with dominoes is a version of sortilege; which is the casting of lots in order to divine the future. The word can be traced to the Anglo-Saxon *hlot* meaning *"allotment"* (*gehlot* meant *"decision"*). Sortilege is one of the most ancient methods of divination. In the Bible there are several mentions of its use. For example, it was used by the sailors to determine whether Jonah was the cause of the tempest (Jonah 1:7): *"And they said every one to his fellow, Come, and let us cast lots, that we may know for whose cause this evil is upon us. So they cast lots and the lot fell upon Jonah."* It was used to determine who should take the place of Judas, in Acts 1:26: *"And they gave forth their lots; and the lot fell upon Matthias; and he was numbered with the eleven apostles."* Also, in Proverbs 16:33 it says: *"The lot is cast into the lap; but the whole disposing thereof is of the Lord."*

Verses taken from books and written on discs, is one form of sortilege. These discs are then strung together and thrown down on the ground. The revealed verses are then the pertinent ones. At Præneste (Palestrina), Italy, the oracle of Fortuna had a number of oak tablets kept in a chest. Fortuna (*identified with the Greek goddess Tyche*), was the Roman goddess of Fate, Chance, and Luck. Each of the oak tablets was inscribed with signs and symbols. When the oracle was consulted, an acolyte would draw-out one of the tablets, at random, from the chest. This would then be interpreted by the priest. Such drawing of lots could only be done on certain days of the year, at Præneste.

The basic form of sortilege is for objects, such as stones, bones, sticks, and dice, to be thrown down after being mixed or shaken together. Their relationship on landing is interpreted, as may be the area where they land (*which might be subdivided into pertinent sections*). The face of the object, or the revealed color or symbol which lands uppermost, is also significant. Black and white beans are sometimes used, as are small bones, dice, sticks of different lengths, and stones. Methods vary.

There are some classical forms of sortilege, such as Sortes Thriæcæ, which is a Greek form where pebbles or counters are thrown into an urn and then one is drawn out. They each have individual signs, letters, or symbols of some sort, marked on them. This form of divination received its name from the Thriæ; three nymphs who nursed Apollo and were said to have invented the system.

There is also Sortes Viales, or *"street lots."* This was used in both Greece and Rome. In this system, a person carried a number of marked lots and walked about in a market place. A young boy encountered by chance, would be asked to draw one of the lots and that would be the infallible prophecy. According to Plutarch (*the Greek writer and biographer; 46-120 ce*), this method came from the Egyptians. A variation on it was for a boy to set-up in a market place, with a tablet covered in possible answers to questions. When consulted, the boy would cast dice on the tablet and read the verses on which they fell. A variation was for various verses to be written on pieces of paper, which were thrown into an urn. The verse drawn out was then the significant one. Albius Tibullus (*c.19BCE*), the Roman poet, wrote of this when he said:

> *"Thrice in the streets the sacred lots she threw,*
> *And thrice the boy a happy omen drew."*

Sortes Prenestinæ, or the Prenestine Lots, were used in Italy. Letters of the alphabet were written on individual tiles and placed in an urn. After mixing, they were turned out on the ground and any words which were accidentally formed by the letters were taken as omens. So it was basically, *"omens by anagrams."*

"Throwsticks" were used during the Archaic Period of ancient Egypt. These were tubular sticks about nine inches long, made from split reeds, though some were of wood or ivory. One face was slightly concave and plain while the other face was convex and decorated. They were thrown down in sets of four, five or six, and interpreted by the layout of face-up or face-down.

Dominoes, as a means of fortune-telling, are popular with many Gypsies. However, the Roma have a superstition that *"the dotted ivories"* should not be touched on a Monday or a Friday. They also believe that the dominoes should not be consulted *"more than once in a moon's span"* (once a month). And they do believe that the tiles are very prophetic.

Domino tiles, or *"bones,"* are rectangular; twice as long as they are wide. There are twenty-eight in a standard double-six set. Later developments had double-nine and even double-twelve sets. As mentioned, the dominoes represent the combination of two sets of dice and the results obtained with them, plus the addition of blanks.

Reading The Dömínöes

*T*here are several different ways to read dominoes. Which method you use will depend upon whether you wish to give a fun reading — perhaps more for entertainment than anything else — or whether you wish to look deeply into yourself or those about you. Dice, dominoes, runes, and tarot cards have all been used at both extremes. Many people start at the fun end of the spectrum and gradually advance, as they become caught-up in the true meanings found in the tiles, dice, or cards used to focus the psychic energies. Others remain at the fun end, and there's nothing wrong with that. I urge you to experiment; to *"play"* and to research. In some ways dominoes are read in a similar way to dice, but one thing that's unique about them is that they can be used to tell the fortune of more than one person at a time.

On occasion you may ask a question and the chosen tile does not seem to answer it; does not seem remotely to touch upon the query. When this happens (and *it's not possible for every single tile to apply to all possible questions*), then turn up a second domino; even a third if you have to. Don't go to more than three. If your question is still not answered to your satisfaction, then the answer is not to be found at that time. Try again in three day's time.

An alternative to laying-out the tiles on a table is to keep them in a bag and then simply reach into the bag and take one.

With the dots on the dominoes, it's not surprising that numerology can also enter the picture. Adding up the number of dots can give additional information. Full *Numerological Significance* is covered later in this book, but I'll mention here one immediate use of the numbers. They can relate to issues of time — *"When will I inherit the family fortune?" "How long before my employer declares bankruptcy?" "How many miles away should I consider relocating?"* The answers to these types of questions can often be found right on the one domino you've drawn. Here's an example of how it can be used:

Say you've drawn the 4 : 3 tile and you are wondering about a time element. You actually have three numbers to consider: four, three, and seven. Seven, of course, is the sum of four and three. (*If the tile had been, for example, 5 : 6 then there would have been four numbers to consider: five, six, eleven, and two. The two is the sum of the two digits in eleven: 11 = 1+1 = 2.*) With the 4 : 3 tile, then, the numbers might indicate days, weeks, months, even years. Or they could be, for example, the fourth day of the third month; additionally, perhaps, seven years from the reading. There is no set meaning to the numbers, so far as time goes. They basically just give you the possibilities. For fuller interpretations — other than time — see the section on *Numerological Significance.*

In-Depth Dömino Meanings

$\mathcal{S}$omething to keep in mind is that with the dominoes — as with the runes, cards, coins, etc. — you are consulting an oracle. You are not doing casual fortune-telling. (*If such is your desire then use the simple, general-interpretation method given later in this book.*) The dominoes, used for the in-depth readings that follow, give you a deeper insight into your own psyche. They may indicate possible pathways in your future but are just as likely to help you focus on what is happening — perhaps at a deeper level — in your present. They help you to see and to accept the responsibilities that come with life.

I think of it as being the doing of *"the Gods"* which decides what particular tile turns up when doing a reading. Fate? Coincidence? Chance? Unimportant? Unimportant it certainly is not. A particular tile will turn up at the moment you need to hear what it has to say. So ask your question, focus on it, turn over the tile, and read what the Gods have to tell you concerning your query. The interpretations given here come directly from Spirit, in the form of inspirational writing.

NOTE:

For the *In-Depth Readings* that follow, you need only turn over one tile and read it. You can supplement it with a second, if you feel the need, and even a third. I would suggest not trying to include more than three tiles at any one reading. Generally just the one will suffice.

0 / 0

Key Word:
Innocence

Additional meanings:
Choice to be made, purity of heart, freedom, lack of restraint. Beware tendency toward carelessness, vanity, bad judgement.

0 / 0

*I*n innocence is all life reflected. It is an open book; a blank sheet of paper, awaiting the written word. It is still water awaiting the ripple of disturbance, large or small. This domino may be seen in the clear, open sky or in the unvarying, all-absorbing darkness of the night sky. Everything is possible on the blank canvas; the choice is your own.

There is the excitement of what is to come; of what may lie *"just around the corner."* There are choices to be made but nothing to indicate what those choices should be. Innocence implies that there is purity of heart and, therefore, no chance of poor judgement. Yet that very innocence may translate as lack of experience, which could well lead to tragedy. Freedom is to be enjoyed but to be respected. By keeping and focusing on the purity of heart, bad decisions may be avoided.

Beware vanity. Making the right choice(s) is not the be-all and end-all for, having made a decision, it is necessary to follow-through and show your ability to handle all that results from that decision. If all goes well, then there can be a feeling of accomplishment, but that can quickly lead to self-satisfaction and arrogance. Never lose sight of the innocent phase. There is an innate joy, love, and sense of wonder connected to this tile. Don't lose that. Keep everything in perspective

0 / 1

Key Word:

Success

Additional meanings:

Overindulgence, imperfections, mistakes

Numerological value:

1

0 / 1

*T*his is frequently a sign of conflict and social disharmony. There is always the possibility of success and it can be within your grasp if you do not fumble, for this tile is not entirely negative. You must beware saying the wrong thing; boasting and/or claiming that which is patently untrue. There can be emotional instability here, either resulting from the above or as a result of it. There is a feeling of being on the outside looking in, with a burning desire to reverse the situation and to be a part of what is going on. There is a desire for respect and yet an inability to command it. Too aggressive behavior can defeat what you unconsciously desire.

You may feel that you have reached an impasse; that you have gone too far and it is now impossible to reverse things. But you can make use of this stalemate. Take the time to search within yourself and to find that sincerity that lies deep within. If you present it gradually — without flinging it in the face of those with whom you are in conflict — than your sincerity can bring about a turn of fortune. It can bring about the eventual success that you desire.

We all make mistakes. But the wiser person learns from his or her mistakes. When things seem to go wrong, examine the course of events and see if there wasn't some other way you might have handled things, and remember that for next time. Success is always within your grasp — you just need to focus on it then reach out and grasp it.

0 / 2

Key Word:
Family

Additional meanings:
Home, contentment, perfect love, attainment,
bliss . . . but tread cautiously

Numerological value:
2

0 / 2

*T*his is a tile of blessing. It frequently ties-in with family love and harmony. There is success, if not financially at the very least in relationships. Abundance in all things is often indicated.

This tile is a bright omen of what lies ahead, reinforcing what has already been achieved. Many times the appearance of this tile indicates an approaching initiation, in the sense of a new beginning. It might be a new job, it might be relocation, it might be a marriage or business partnership. It signals attainment. You have accomplished more than you ever thought you would or could. There is, however, a caveat: a word of caution. Do not rest on your laurels. Do not think that because you have attained a particular level, there is no need to continue the climb. Always look ahead. *"Onward and upward"* apply here. This is tile of the optimist, not the pessimist.

There is abundance of life reflected here. Procreation, eroticism, pleasure, even birth are in this tile. It is the realization of a dream and the attainment of goals. There are indications of swelling bank accounts; of growing circles of friends; of new interests and horizons. All are within easy reach. They do not have to be accepted, but they are available. Remember always not to stagnate.

0 / 3

Key Word:
Birth

Additional meanings:

Birth of idea, news, new proposal. Trust. Beware tendency toward deception, seduction.

Numerological value:
3

0 / 3

Y ou possess the energy that is found in new birth, in the blossoming of springtime, the flowers bursting forth in a grand array of colors. A new cycle of birth/rebirth and fresh beginnings is here. There is also healing and intuition. As a child enters the world, it must trust in all that has brought it forth, for it takes time to achieve and accept self-responsibility. Only over time will strength develop and new pathways be made. The focus here is on the early steps. There is news of birth; of new life.

You are pointed toward a new way of progress. You will need to prove yourself. You will need to test your strength and fine-tune your judgements. It is said that from small acorns grow mighty oaks. Let this be your inspiration. Know that you have great potential and that for you all things are possible.

A motherly influence can be felt, with this tile. There is gentle nourishment with positive encouragement. Purification may be needed to ensure adherence to the right path. Look for news about an opportunity, proposal, or early investment. This is also a tile that works with feminine energies and with healing powers. To carry this tile, close to the heart, can produce great recuperative energy. It will promote personal well-being, physically and mentally.

0 / 4

Key Word:
Proposition

Additional meanings:

Message, invitation, competition. Beware tendency toward deception, fraud.

Numerological value:
4

0 / 4

*T*here are problems of underachievement and of alienation. Feelings of fraud and trickery may be no more than paranoia, yet it behooves you to take all precautions. Somewhere there has been some misdirection, but it may not have been given deliberately. In fact it may not have been given to you at all but be the result of your own impetuosity. Take time to review your past and possibly re-plan your future. If you are to change then you must first recognize your present situation. Recognize it and accept it. Then set about changing it.

The first thing to do is to acknowledge that there is competition. It cannot all be plain sailing. Know within your heart that you have potential. If you plan well, take your time, and draw on all of your natural abilities, then you can face any competition that comes along. You are not *"special"* for we are all special. It is what we do with our special qualities that makes the difference.

There is someone you know — possibly someone close to you — who is frustrated from perceived roadblocks in his or her life. There is great ambition there but no progress seems to have been made. Give encouragement and, where possible, lend a helping hand. You may receive an invitation or offer which looks promising. Don't be too quick to refuse and, although caution is advised, don't treat the invitation or offer with too much suspicion.

0 / 5

Key Word:

Nurturing

Additional meanings:

Visionary gift, poetry, imagination, pleasure, generosity.

Numerological value:

5

0 / 5

With this tile, there is a connection to an older, wise woman who can be trusted in all things. She is a source of unconditional love and encouragement. This is the person to whom you can turn in any and all emotional affairs and situations. She will never laugh at you or ridicule you. She will help guide you through words of wisdom, to which you should listen carefully.

If you are unable to equate this tile with any particular person then it may be that it is indicating a safe haven that is at hand; a situation you may place yourself in that will bring about this needed love and encouragement. By searching your mind you will be able to recognize the direction in which you are being pointed, leading to the feelings of security you need at this time.

Poetry is reflected in this tile. The musical poetry of rhyme and rhythm that calms, soothes, and lulls you into a feeling of safety and self-assurance is found here. This is an excellent tile to use for meditation. Study it, reflect on it, use it as a starting point from which your mind may launch itself into gentle introspection. It is a tool of the imagination that can bring great pleasure and lead to escape from that which may have been acting negatively on you.

Re-acquaint yourself with some of the music of your younger days; the quieter, contemplative variety rather than the louder and celebratory type.

0 / 6

Key Word:

Generosity

Additional meanings:

Quiet power, and responsibility; lawyer, balance.
Beware tendency toward injustice, scandal, lawsuit

Numerological value:

6

0 / 6

*T*his tile is the male equivalent of 0 : 5 for it embodies the quiet power found in a solid figure who has journeyed long and far to arrive at his present position. He is wise yet compassionate; a kind, fatherly figure who willingly shares with those who have need of his knowledge. Whether or not you understand him is immaterial; just know that you can trust him. (Again as with 0 : 5, *if you're unable to equate this tile with any particular person then it may be that it is indicating a situation you may place yourself in that will bring about needed love and encouragement.*)

You need to listen to the advice offered by an older male (or an *established institute*). Initially you may feel that you do not need the advice; that you are quite capable of solving your own problems. But here is someone who has *"been there; done that"*! Let the voice of experience save you from much trial and tribulation. It is possible that this figure is connected with the law, in the sense of being a lawyer or attorney. The figure of justice — blindfolded and holding up a balance — is present behind this person. By listening to what this man has to say, you could avoid the possibility of scandal and even a lawsuit.

Yet as with all things, you must make up your own mind for the final decision. You are the one who is affected and who will have to live with the results of your decision. Listen to all offered advice, weigh it carefully, then make up your own mind and proceed with certainty.

1 / 0

Key Word:

Sudden advancement

Additional meanings:

Haste, end of a journey, swift messenger, freedom of action.

Numerological value:

1

1 / 0

*S*uddenly all obstacles have been pushed aside. You can move ahead at a good speed. What had seemed potentially threatening, if not downright dangerous, has now been hindered, perhaps even totally removed. You have absolute freedom of action. Now is the time to quickly review your past plans — those that you may have put to one side thinking them unworkable. In the light of this newfound freedom, consider all of your options and lose no time in moving forward.

This is an excellent tile when considering finances, especially in the sense of investments and enterprise. Moving forward now will ensure continuing advancement in the future. Act as though the window of opportunity is for a limited time only, in this way you will not lose the impetus that has been given you. Firm-up your plan of action and put it into play just as quickly as possible. Yet don't overlook anything; make sure that the plan is sound.

This tile can apply equally to the romantic side of your life. Again, move forward and act. What you had only dreamed of is now within your grasp. Support and cooperation will materialize as you need them.

You have done work in the past which can now be built upon. You have laid the foundations for events that can now begin to take shape. Now is the time to start growing; to begin expanding and developing as you've always wanted to.

1 / 1

Key Word:
Preparedness

Additional meanings:
Strength in reserve, defense, hidden foes

Numerological values:
1, 2

1 / 1

*I*n order to prepare, you must stop doing what you were doing and concentrate on the preparation for what lies ahead. You cannot properly prepare for something if you are absorbed in another activity at the same time. So stop, relax, and think about what lies ahead. At the moment time is most precious. Plan your time carefully. If necessary draw-up a timetable of essential activities, leaving yourself time for detailed planning and preparation.

There may be those who, for whatever reasons, wish to delay you or even prevent you from reaching your goal. Because of this it would behoove you to keep an eye open and be alert for any indication of a developing problem, so that you can face it immediately and deal with it.

A further meaning of this tile is the loss of someone close, whether through death or other means. It indicates closure, and closure that is complete; there is no going back. Knowing this, if you encounter the termination of what had previously seemed an open path, don't waste time and energy on trying to reverse it. Instead, put all your energies into proceeding in a new and more fruitful direction. This tile can also indicate news of a past friend — someone you haven't seen in many years — or the return of old problems.

You may have been wounded or hurt in some way, but you still have all your faculties and are still able to swing into action if and when necessary. This is a time when you feel tired and would dearly love to lie down and rest, but there is much to do and you must remain vigilant.

1 / 2

Key Word:

Overload

Additional meanings:

*Temporary burden, overreaching,
success through extra effort*

Numerological values:

1, 2, 3

1 / 2

You can become very frustrated, and extremely tired, if you try to fight against the way things are going at the moment. You are being swept along and it's useless to try to fight against it. You feel you are overloaded and desperately want to stop and rest, but events are moving too fast. The more you try to change them and the more you try to steer things in a different direction, the more you feel yourself going out of control.

The answer is to stop fighting. Not to give up, but to relax and take time to regain your strength and get your bearings. This is a good time to meditate. Clear your head of all the problems; of all the many things pressing in on you at the moment. Let them flow over you. Go with that flow. Instead of fighting to swim upstream, as it were, turn around and let yourself float downstream. Center yourself and let things be.

You can easily overextend yourself at this time by unnecessarily struggling to go in the direction you want to go. Acknowledge that it's going to take a lot longer than you thought, and wished, to reach your destination. The best thing you can do right now is to conserve your strength and plan ahead.

This tile also may indicate that you are being very insensitive to someone at this time. You are unconsciously hurting someone you care about. Perhaps you are being too strict; adhering to values which need revising. Or you might be preoccupied and not giving enough attention to someone or some situation. Review your responsibilities and see if you are being remiss in any duties. Then review your own handling of recent situations and relationships. It's not too late to make amends.

1 / 3

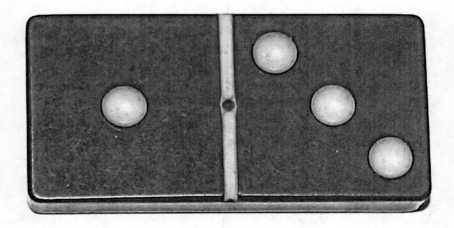

Key Word:
Messenger

Additional meanings:
Envoy, good or bad news, instability, indecision

Numerological values:
1, 3, 4

1 / 3

*T*his tile is associated with family and the home. There may be a quarrel within the family that could split the unit; a major domestic dispute. Try to avoid stubbornness at this time and put yourself in the other person's place. Try to see their point of view. Diplomacy is preferable to a break-down of relationships. A lack of trust may be at the root of this dispute. Sit down and work out some ground rules that will negate any such lack of trust in the future. Draw-up safeguards and guidelines. There may be a question of privacy, or lack of it. This can be a mountain that has grown out of a molehill. Each side must be willing to give a little to solve the major problem.

This tile also indicates the coming of news that would seem to be a help with financial problems. However, the news is not to be trusted. Hesitation may result and time is of the essence. If there is any doubt about the validity of what is presented, then sit down and use pencil and paper, if necessary, to work out the pros and the cons; to compare the possible results depending upon the actions you might take. This is a time for careful evaluation. Don't make any hasty decisions.

Beware of living beyond your means. It may seem easy to put some charge on a credit card, or similar, but that still leaves the bill to be paid . . . if not now, then later. Small charges can add up, leading to large bills that need to be paid. This is a time to be frugal. Put off the purchase of anything that is not absolutely essential. You can survive without decorative objects, without purely personal items, without those things that simply enhance. There will be time enough to add all of these later. For now — be financially cautious.

1 / 4

Key Word:

Relocation

Additional meanings:

Flight, absence, journey, resistance to success

Numerological values:

1, 4, 5

1 / 4

*T*here is a trusted and faithful friend apparent in this tile. He or she is there to give strength and to aid you in what you are about to undertake. There is the possibility of relocation or of travel for you, and this friend will help you prepare for it in some positive way. The friend is young, but not without experience. Plan carefully, but there may be unexpected delays. If such a friend does not exist, then know that you have the inner strength necessary to carry you forward, through any obstacles that may arise.

This is a time to repay old debts. You need to mend some fences. There are those from whom you have borrowed in the past without really acknowledging their aid and efforts. You have been taking them for granted. Now is the time to draw-in these past overdue accounts. You have long been resisting this balancing of life's books but it's time to face up to it.

You have for some time been feeling that you are a victim, yet you have a vast amount of inner strength in reserve that can protect you and ensure that you are never truly victimized. You have a tendency to think about running away from your problems, yet to run away is to turn your back on new opportunities. There are paths leading to success that may be missed if you turn aside.

1 / 5

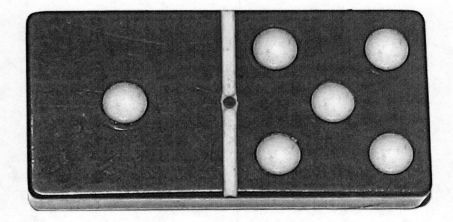

Key Word:

honor

Additional meanings:

Home-loving, passion, nature lover. Beware tendency toward jealousy.

Numerological values:

1, 5, 6

1/5

*T*his is the tile of honor, both as a noun and as a verb. In other words, it is both the honor you have and it is also the act of honoring others. You are generally very supportive of those closest to you, especially when they are going through hard times. You are happy to share your knowledge and skills, to help others.

This is a time to stop hesitating and to take positive action. This is especially true where life — animal, vegetable and mineral — is concerned. If you were to join an environmental group, or other positive action organization, you would discover that you receive far more from your efforts than you could ever have believed.

First order is to survey your attitudes. This includes not only your attitudes to other people but also to the environment. For example, do you — or have you ever — used items that would damage the environment? Do you use sprays, weed-killers or the like, that can be damaging? Do you recycle? Are you a noise polluter? Do you litter? You receive what you give out and should constantly be aware of how you may appear to others.

All of this can apply equally well in the metaphorical rather than the literal sense. For example, are you a *"polluter"* in terms of what you say — perhaps indulging in harmful gossip and making unthinking and even insulting remarks about others. A negative attitude toward others and constant anti-social behavior in public situations can be as polluting as littering and the use of toxic chemicals.

This is also a time to focus on the home. Stop putting-off those many little jobs that need to be done. Make your home appear beautiful on both the outside and the inside. There is a tendency to neglect the inside of the home through familiarity with it. Take the time to straighten-up, clean, and refresh. Add flowers and keep plants well watered. Clean windows and put away untidy piles of clothes, papers, or anything else that has been left lying around. Develop a pride in the appearance of your surroundings.

1 / 6

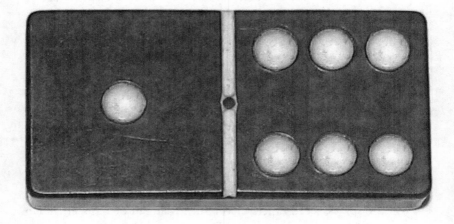

Key Word:

Conscientiousness

Additional meanings:

Honesty, nobility; inheritance. Beware tendency toward severity, stern judgements

Numerological values:

1, 6, 7

1 / 6

*T*here is a person or a situation in your life where success and power are especially influential. Yet this success and power are presented in a conscientious manner, for your good and the good of those about you. If this is a person, then he or she can be a trusted ally and a good friend. Trust any advice received. Counsel is especially valuable when it concerns finances, investing, and real estate.

This is a time when you need to be scrupulously honest both with yourself and in your dealings with others. It would help to keep in your mind a feeling of nobility; a mental association with those who are in positions of responsibility and who manage all affairs with wisdom, fairness, and kindness. Your financial position has nothing to do with this attitude; it is one of applying yourself in your dealings with those with whom you come in contact. This is a time to demonstrate your strength of character.

This is also a good time to expand your circle of friends. Look for new experiences; new interests. Join clubs and volunteer for organizations. If asked to help at any function, accept immediately. Many times casual contact through such activities can lead to long-lasting friendships and/or benefits that may affect your life in a variety of ways. Open up your mind and your heart to others and to new ideas and activities.

2 / 0

Key Word:
Crisis

Additional meanings:

Bondage, paralysis, indecision, difficulties. But be prepared for release, relaxation, and new beginnings

Numerological values:
2

2/0

You have chosen to look on the dark side rather than to acknowledge challenges and seek the light. This is the tile of the pessimist, not the optimist. You are on the verge of losing control, if you have not already done so. It is a time of crisis. You feel that events are overwhelming you, yet you should not allow them to paralyze you. Acknowledge that there are difficulties but center yourself, relax, and give yourself time to sort out the details. You need to meditate; to ground yourself and lose the feeling of dread. There are ways out; there are new beginnings possible; there are methods of release, if you take the time to look for them and use them.

This can be a creative block. You may feel that you have run dry of ideas and don't know which way to turn. The harder you try, the worse things seem to be and the more you are drawn toward panic. Stop! Relax. Breathe deeply and give yourself time to recover. Do not turn to alcohol, drugs, or any form of artificial stimulant at this time. Your release lies in cleansing your system, both physically and mentally.

You may be allowing others to take control of your life, by letting them manipulate you. Unconsciously you are aware of this but consciously you are doing nothing to fight it. You need to stand up for yourself. Speak out when there is a need, instead of allowing things to go unsaid. Resist being forced into situations that you know are not good for you. Question authority. Remember the old expression *"It's always darkest before the dawn."* Know, then, that dawn is on its way and move toward it.

A friendship or relationship of some sort may be dying. You need to face up to the situation and decide whether or not to act. Is the relationship worth saving? How has it reached this point? Was there something you could have done to prevent it? If so, is it too late? If there is change and you are aware of it, then you can have control of it.

2 / 1

Key Word:
Desolation

Additional meanings:

*Despair, failure, inability to decide, suffering.
Beware tendency toward shame, fear, doubt.*

Numerological values:
1, 2, 3

2 / 1

*T*his can be a very negative tile, if you let it be. It is associated with failure and despair. But most failure is the result of despair. It doesn't always have to be. If you can get through this phase then you will be the stronger for it. There is the chance here to seek out and correct weaknesses in your life and in your plans for the future. Depression may keep you from seeing positive possibilities.

You may have experienced repeated failures to the point where you feel that everyone and everything is working against you. You have arrived at a mental state where you are now placing blockages in your own mind, because of it. You have tried to handle too much alone. Now is the time to seek help and guidance from others. Ask advice of those you feel you can trust. Fight any feelings that you *"know it all"* and acknowledge that there are those who are better able to see the whole picture and, from their perspective, are able to offer advice that will be sound. Don't let pride keep you from victory. There is no need to feel fear or shame. You may not be willing to admit that anything is wrong, yet unconsciously you know it is. Face up to it and deal with it.

2 / 2

Key Word:
Misfortune

Additional meanings:
Pain, affliction, extreme burdens, defeat, possible ruin.

Numerological values:
2, 4

2/2

*T*his tile runs the gamut from a short spell of bad luck to absolute disaster. It can especially influence your financial stability. You may be losing what you had gained long ago or there may be a sudden reversal of fortune so that as soon as you achieve some success there is an immediate failure and loss. If there is any lesson to be learned from this, it is to not cling to possessions.

Possessions can take over and possess the owner. *"He who dies with the most toys, wins"* is a poor motto, for you cannot take them with you. Allow things to flow into your life but be equally ready to see them flow out again. Don't put emphasis on ownership but on the experience of ownership. Learn from having what you own and know that ownership may be only temporary. If you get caught up in the fact that you are suffering losses, then you will experience pain and suffer feelings of failure and potential ruin. But by focusing more on what you may learn from the passing assets, you will benefit and be able to apply your experience to the future. There may be temporary frustration, but it will pass if you do not cling. You may feel helpless as you watch what you have loved and cherished evaporate, but know that everything can, in time, be replaced.

There may be false starts and lack of initiative, with feelings of inadequacy and ineffectiveness. Examine your thoughts and your actions. Much of what is happening may be the result of you holding onto things that you should be sharing with others. Look for those who may need to learn from you and extend energy to them. By helping others you may end up helping yourself.

We create our own reality. When we suffer misfortune — especially a lot of misfortune, with one event after another — it is a sign that we need to *"pull back and regroup"*. We need to reassess our position in life and our goals, especially our long term goals. Think positive and aim high. If you determine that you do not have to endure pain and suffering, then you can eliminate it. Create a reality that is positive, and then live it.

2 / 3

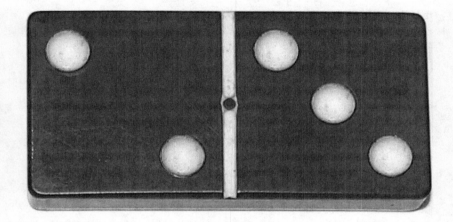

Key Word:
Secrecy

Additional meanings:

Espionage, vigilance, unexpected events.
Beware tendency toward possible illness.

Numerological values:

2, 3, 5

2/3

*T*here is an inherent weakness which needs to be addressed. It's reflected in a lack of effort in many of the things undertaken. *"Half-hearted"* is an applicable word. You may have an initial enthusiasm for a project which quickly dissipates, and you become either bored or detracted by another possible path. This lack of enthusiasm can frequently lead to missed opportunities which otherwise would have been very beneficial for you. You also tend toward secrecy; not letting others know what you are involved in and, once again, missing opportunities where offers may have been made had others known of your interests.

There is a resistance to change, even when it is obvious that the change would be beneficial. If you are to keep on top of things and to advance as you would like, you need to keep your ears and eyes open and to seize opportunities when they arise. Nothing is going to flow into you naturally; you need to go out and seize all that you can. It's time to stir; to set goals and to vigorously pursue them.

There is a complementary weakness in your physical make-up that could lead to illness. You tend to dismiss indications of need for medication and if you do start administering something, will not persevere with it. At this time you may expect some minor illness, if it is not already in evidence.

There may be deceit evident at this time. You should examine carefully any important papers — especially contracts — before signing them. Double-check balance sheets, bills, and store receipts. There may even be someone working against you in some way, trying to undermine your plans.

2 / 4

Key Word:

Bravery

Additional meanings:

Imprudence, extravagance, false bravado.

Numerological values:

2, 4, 6

2/4

*A*lthough this tile is associated with bravery, it more often indicates a need for bravery; reflecting a false bravado. You may talk a good fight, but when the chips are down your motto is more likely to be *"Those who fight and run away, live to fight another day."* There is some truth in that saying, but not when it might mean leaving others to finish the fight for you.

There may also be an indication, at this time, of a misuse or even perversion of knowledge. This is not necessarily coming from you. You must be on your toes to be aware of any false representation made by anyone with whom you come into contact. You must also make a point of being scrupulously honest in all your own dealings with others. Be aware of gossip, and don't repeat what you cannot verify.

Make sure you listen to advise when it is offered. You have a tendency to dismiss good advice, often simply because you hadn't thought of it yourself. You are more inclined to plod along — frequently *"re-inventing the wheel"* — rather than accepting the results obtained by others. You need to be less suspicious, yet still keep a wary eye on the possible intent of others.

You can easily become restless and impatient at the present time. Make yourself relax and allow things to follow their natural line without forcing issues. Be careful in whom you place your trust; there may be a younger person who is overly ambitious and working against you.

2 / 5

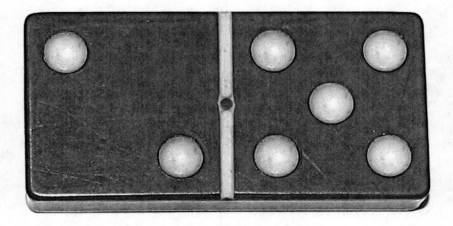

Key Word:

Perception

Additional meanings:

Sadness, mourning. Beware tendency toward malice, bigotry, deceit

Numerological values:

2, 5, 7

2 / 5

*T*here is a woman of power, position and authority, who can bring great sadness to you at this time. She seems selfishly incapable of relating to others and to the unexpected negativity that may enter their lives. If not an actual woman, this may be a situation that has arisen, perhaps with a federal or local government body, or similar. You will need to have all your facts and documents in hand, for simply relating your impressions will carry no weight. Your best interests will not be served without a long, and possibly costly, struggle. Do not lie to get what you want, for your lies would be uncovered and your situation made worse.

You may have made an error, or errors, in judgement. You may have trusted the wrong person. You may have put all your money on the wrong horse, metaphorically speaking (or perhaps literally!). Expect delays, both in travel and in the course of events. There is no sense in growing impatient because things are going to take as long as they need to. In the case of travel, there is the possibility of delays, cancellations, lost baggage, flat tires, and all such unexpected inconveniences. But accept them for what they are inconveniences. Nothing is to be gained by becoming angry and upset. Practice patience and always try to see the humorous side of any situation.

There may be an unexpected change of direction in your life. You may seem to have lost your impetus and find yourself meandering like a ship without a rudder, at the mercy of the winds and the currents. You don't seem to be making any headway and are not moving forward toward your established goals. Now is the time to reassign your goals; to review your path in life. Pull back and take this time to plan, rather than trying to force your way ahead.

2/6

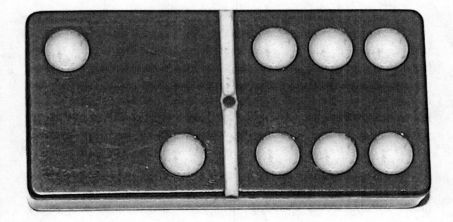

Key Word:

Wisdom

Additional meanings:

*Authority, justice, power,
perception, strong will.*

Numerological values:

2, 6, 8

2/6

Wisdom comes from opening-up and receiving. By listening, reading, observing, and mentally noting the actions and behavior of others, wisdom accrues and with it, power.

This tile indicates a person, or an authority, of great intelligence and influence presently in your life. This person, organization, or simply a situation, exercises a lot of control over your speech and actions; indeed over all your activities. Although you may find it comforting to have such a backing, at times it can become stifling and restrictive.

There is unpredictability to the present situation. Many times decisions are made that might be positive to the majority of people involved but which do not necessarily suit you nor advance you in the best way possible. You sometimes yearn for more independence, to make your own decisions and guide your own life. You frequently find yourself having to compromise when you would far rather make a definite and distinctive decision. There is no room for spontaneity, in your present situation. It contains energy far greater than your own. Exercise caution.

You must find the wisdom, and the strength of purpose, to act on your own behalf. By reviewing your life experiences you can find, within yourself, that which will set your feet on the right path and lead you to the end that you seek. Be adaptable; be willing to make changes; keep your eyes and ears open for opportunities. Respond to challenges as rapidly as possible but not without long-delaying thought. Enter all situations with a *"worst case scenario"* action already planned and plotted. Know that whatever happens is all part of life's experience and from it, you can learn.

3 / 0

Key Word:
𝔖kill

Additional meanings:

Craftsmanship, apprenticeship, learning, creation.
Beware tendency toward vanity and immodesty.

Numerological values:
3

3 / 0

This is the tile of skill, but skill that must be carefully balanced. Note the warning to beware a tendency to vanity and immodesty. It might also say boastfulness. To have a skill implies a time (perhaps a long time) of study and practice. Patience is implicit. Many skills include an apprenticeship where the operator serves a certain period being taught by an acknowledged master; assiduously learning and practicing. Once learned, there is a period of building experience, leading to later creation of personal characteristics.

This tile infers all the above, showing that you are well along the path that will take you to being accomplished in some field. The main thing you must do at this time is keep your mind open and receptive. There is a great deal to be learned. If you considered it all at once, it would seem overwhelming and you would be discouraged. You must remember to take things one day at a time. Remember the tortoise and the hare. Slowness but persistence is what wins the race.

Pride has a place in workmanship. You should be proud of all that you do and all that you achieve. You must, however, be on guard against boastfulness. There is a fine line between the two. Let others praise you, but don't hesitate to offer your work for approval and any structural criticism.

3 / 1

Key Word:

Accomplishment

Additional meanings:

**Material success. Beware tendency toward
deception and bad faith.**

Numerological values:

1, 3, 4

3/1

You seem to be doing well financially and are enjoying some success, but beware. Bad luck and depression can easily become a part of life. Risks are being taken when they shouldn't be. There is a sense of accomplishment but it is very tenuous. Hopes are frequently dashed. Material success seems at hand yet frequently slips away. Be very careful that you don't fall into debt. It's easy to use a credit card, thinking you can quickly pay it off, but delays to that repayment can bring unexpected and unnecessary high interest rates.

Don't take any chances at this time; financially, in your personal life, and especially not with your health. Don't lend money to friends, it can be the beginning of the end of that friendship.

This is a time to try a new angle on things. The old ways will no longer work. Think out new strategies for your business and personal life. This is not the moment to be trying to up-grade, be it with real estate, automobile, office space, or whatever. Your energies are very easily scattered at this time and you need to focus them. Establish a new game plan and put all your energy into it. Right now don't focus too much on the end result you want to achieve but work on the details of the steps to getting there.

You may feel overwhelmed and tempted to simply give up. Don't. If you are exhausted, then take a few moments every day to meditate and to recharge your batteries. Know that you cannot achieve everything at once; some things take time. Acknowledge this and don't push yourself beyond your limits.

This is an ideal time to bring into play your sense of humor. Whenever possible, when things go wrong step back and look at them, seeing possible humor in the situation. Laugh at yourself; laugh at what is happening; laugh and learn.

3 / 2

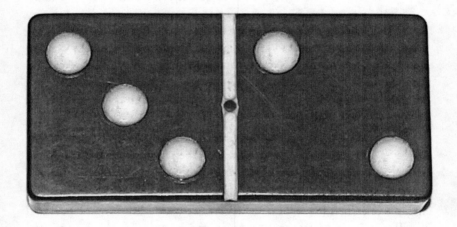

Key Word:
Inheritance

Additional meanings:
Real estate, family matters, prosperity.

Numerological values:
2, 3, 5

3 / 2

*T*his tile represents rewards; returns for hard work. It is usually something you have been expecting to receive. But what you receive, you must use to help others as well as yourself. Family is important and you must acknowledge that.

There has been some success in recent situations. You may feel confident, content and secure; firmly established in your position. Family matters are going well and — in addition to earned rewards, or as an alternate — there is the possibility of an inheritance, if not financial then one of situation *(possibly a relocation, promotion, raise, or similar)*.

This is definitely a tile associated with financial success; expected or unexpected monetary gain. It may also signify the fulfillment of love. If there has been any sense of loneliness, this will come to an end. If you have been searching for the ideal partner, then one will be found.

Remain vigilant and mindful. To have riches is to be aware of others' desires to take them from you. Be generous and, in so doing, you will take the edge off any feelings of envy by others. Enjoy yourself but don't allow yourself to become ostentatious.

Conserve what you have gained. Don't keep your money in cash under the mattress! *(Some do.)* Put it into a bank account where it will not only be safe but will also draw interest. If you decide to invest, then invest wisely and carefully and keep a close eye on the progress of where you have invested.

On the spiritual path, this is an excellent time to acknowledge the divine. Your mind is open and you can be in touch with Spirit in its many forms. This is a good time to work on psychic development. If you don't already, adopt a regimen of daily meditation.

3 / 3

Key Word:

Reflection

Additional meanings:

Scholarship, study, news, concentration. Beware tendency toward wastefulness.

Numerological values:

3, 6

3 / 3

*A*t the present time there are negative energies about you. There is disharmony around you bringing about quarreling and disputes of various sorts. There is suspicion, which may or may not be justified.

Try not to hang on to feelings of hurt and discontent. Let go off grudges. By involving yourself in study — reading, taking a course, learning a language — you can allow much of this negativity to by-pass you. This is an excellent time to study. Meditate; take time to reflect, relax and wind down.

Expect news to arrive. This could be good or bad but it is coming from an unexpected source. It may be from someone you haven't heard from in many years or it may be someone you do not know but who is acquainted with a mutual friend. The news will be unusual, possibly throwing you off balance for a short time. Don't act on it right away. Give yourself time to absorb it and to put it into perspective.

There may be someone coming into your life at this time who needs to learn from you. He or she is not greatly concerned with practical matters and needs to be shown how to ground and how to fit-in with society. This person tends to fight against convention and enjoys being *"different"* just for the sake of being different. They may need to learn that there are times more appropriate for rebellion than those often chosen.

3 /4

Key Word:
Responsibility

Additional meanings:
Patience, reliability, dependability.
Beware tendency toward idleness and carelessness.

Numerological values:
3, 4, 7

3/4

You are anxious for new beginnings and have some ideas on where you want to go in life but right now there are distractions and interferences. It seems difficult to get things started and when you do, they seem to flounder and fail. You need to look at the environment in which you work. It may need to be changed. You need something to bring new verve, vivacity and excitement into your everyday life. It may be no more than redecorating — perhaps painting the walls — or it may be a major relocation.

You must accept responsibility that you have been avoiding for a long time. You need to show yourself as a person who is dependable and reliable. You can't afford to be careless or others will move in and push you out of the way. There are some tough decisions ahead of you but you have the ability to make them and follow-through with them.

There is a powerful and negative mother-figure, or a *"mothering type"* of situation, that needs to be faced. There could also be difficulties with a particular branch of the family. At this time some old ties may be broken, which will be emotional for you at the time but will later prove to be better for you. There are some tough decisions to be made.

You could become careless at this time so pay attention to what you are doing and especially to details. Be careful that you don't become lazy; putting off till tomorrow what you feel needn't be done today. Get it done now and then it's out of the way.

3 / 5

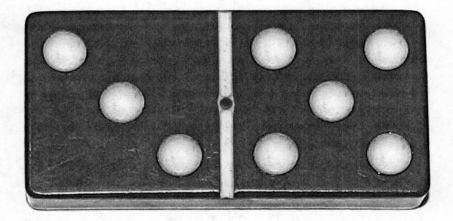

Key Word:

Generosity

Additional meanings:

*Thoughtfulness, freedom from material possessions.
Beware tendency toward suspicion; distrust.*

Numerological values:

3, 5, 8

3 / 5

*T*his tile indicates that there is much work ahead but that it will be made easier in cooperation with others. You should be generous of your time and energy, to reach the goal established. This is not the time to stand idly watching as events pass you by.

This is a time for possible change in your life, whether it be travel, a change of occupation, or a relocation. It might also indicate a change of status from single to married, or even the reverse. Whichever it is, the change will be for the better. The physical part of moving will be a part of it: moving boxes, furniture, possessions of one sort or another. This, along with travel.

This is a good time to thin-out your possessions; a good time to whittle them down to the bare essentials. Give freely to others. Stop holding-on to items simply to possess them. Collections can grow without you being aware of them. Now is the time to break-up those collections and disperse the separate items.

There may be a wise and loving woman in the picture, whose advice you would do well to follow. She may offer financial help, if it is needed. If so, pay no heed to feelings of distrust or doubt that you may have. This would be a genuine offer to help, made by someone well able to afford it. This person would be a wonderful and valuable friend to have, so develop the friendship. She has no ulterior motive but genuinely wants to help you move ahead in your life. (It may be that this is not a single woman but a group or a situation that can advance you.)

3/6

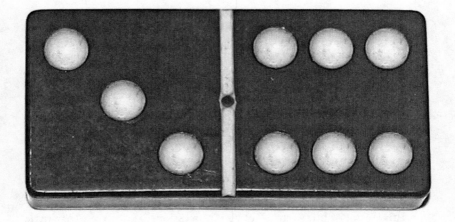

Key Word:

Valor

Additional meanings:

Intelligence, mathematical ability. Beware of tendency toward vice and corruption.

Numerological values:

3, 6, 9

3/6

You may be in a vulnerable position, with threatening influences about you. You are unprotected but, with vigilance, can guard against any potential problems. Things seem very insecure at this time. Finances are precarious; relationships are in the balance; job security is an issue. This calls for determination and boldness on your part.

Keep your eyes and your ears open but, at the same time, do not develop paranoia. Carefully examine anything that you perceive as a possible threat, recognizing that not everything is against you. However, do examine, very carefully, any contracts presented to you at this time, also any business arrangements and even personal relationships. Do not fall into the trap of fighting dishonesty and corruption with the same or similar tactics. Two wrongs do not make a right. There is dishonesty about you but don't you become a part of it.

Be on your guard against giving away your power to others. There may be an older, powerful man who is in the picture and can influence you. Approach him with great care and do not trust him implicitly. Appearances can be deceiving. There is a time to fall back on trust based on intuition, but this is not it. Check and double-check everything presented to you, for there is the strong possibility of dishonesty at work. Don't be afraid to refuse something which, on the surface, seems the answer to a prayer. Let time work for you, and make time for other less threatening offers to appear. The horizon may appear dark, but there is light just beyond it.

4 / 0

Key Word:

Enlightenment

Additional meanings:

Mastery, occult knowledge, skill, wisdom.
The ability to control others and to direct power.
Beware tendency toward insecurity.

Numerological values:

4

4 / 0

*T*his is the domino of enlightenment brought about by occult knowledge, skill and wisdom. There may well be a link to a past life or lives, with the accumulation of experiences contributing to the present mastery. There is also a tapping-in to the universal consciousness.

The main aspect of this tile is to receive knowledge. This is more a time to accept and accumulate rather than to teach and dispense knowledge. A steady regimen of meditation is called for, with thoughtful entries in a personal journal being a useful adjunct. You may experience a number of cases of déjà vu. Do not dismiss them as pure coincidence. They are there for a purpose — perhaps to align your mind in a particular direction, to bring back past-life memories that are pertinent to your life today.

This is a good time to begin a course in self-improvement, psychic development, Spiritualism, healing, or similar. Open yourself to new knowledge and experiences. Acknowledge that you can learn a lot from others. Take the time to read as much as you can, perhaps focusing on non-fiction, self-improvement books. This is not a time to focus on possessions but on spiritual matters.

You do have the ability and knowledge to make great headway along the path you have chosen in life. You posses many talents and abilities and are highly regarded by others, whether or not you are aware of it. But now is the moment to spend time on yourself and your own advancement. Develop those skills you possess. Review your goal(s) in life and the steps to achieving it. Open your mind to your Higher Self and accept the advice that is given. If you give out anything, let it be pure love.

4 / 1

Key Word:

Practicality

Additional meanings:

Objectivity, wisdom, sagacity; hidden influences at work. Beware a tendency toward short-sightedness.

Numerological values:

1, 4, 5

4 / 1

*T*his is a tile of wisdom and understanding. You have knowledge which you can share with others, to their benefit. Whether your life thus far has been long or short, you are an *"old soul"* and, as such, have a vast amount of experience and wisdom to impart. There are certain *"mysteries"* which you have, locked deep within you. By opening-up your mind, through meditation or similar, you can reveal these mysteries, not only to yourself but also to others.

You may find yourself in the position of teacher. Do not allow yourself to become a guru, in the sense of feeling that you have to be all-knowing. You have much to offer but there are still many things which you do not know or understand. Have the humility to acknowledge that. Don't be afraid to say *"I don't know."*

This tile also indicates the strong possibility of travel: short trips and long journeys. These will help educate you, bringing you new knowledge and enlightenment. However, avoid aimless wandering and of travel just for the sake of traveling. Your trips and journeys will frequently tie-in with your mundane work and everyday life. There will be business trips that are so much more than that, and planned vacation trips that develop into far broader excursions. Let these travels help expand your mind and lead you to further investigation through reading and audio-visual research.

There is the possibility of your travel being on the astral plane; of out-of-body experiences that educate and broaden your horizons. If you do not already do so, keep a notebook and pencil at your bedside and, immediately upon awakening, write down all that you remember of your dreams. Do not delay, taking time for a cup of coffee or the like, but write down what you can recall as soon as your eyes open. This Dream Journal will gradually grow into a balanced and informative diary of your astral journeys.

4 / 2

Key Word:

Fertility

Additional meanings:

Home, children, union

Numerological values:

2, 4, 6

4 / 2

*T*his domino is the tile of the family. It relates to the family unit: spouse and off-spring, homestead and immediate surroundings. It covers a house, an apartment, a tent, a mobile home; whichever is the home of the enquirer.

The emphasis of this tile is on happiness in the home. There is comfort in the home state. It is a safe haven from the rigors of the outside world. Returning home after a time away *"recharges the batteries"* of the soul. It is a place where all barriers can be lowered and where body and soul can relax and let go.

Along with the above is an interest in environmental issues. The Earth is our home; the home of all life. As such, it deserves respect and should be honored. This is a good time to get involved with environmental action groups; a good time for recycling and awareness of others' damage and pollution. On a smaller scale, it can benefit you to clean out your personal space, getting rid of unnecessary items by donating them to worthwhile causes and individuals.

Marriage, close friendships, children, expansion of interests are all a part of this tile. This is a fertile time for developing all areas of your life. It can also apply to business and your professional life. This would be a good time to enter into a partnership, open a new branch, add a new room, or simply expand on your advertising.

Open your mind to cooperation with others. Sharing — giving out and taking in — can be beneficial to all concerned. Now is a good time to work with others, moving forward together rather than working as rivals.

4 / 3

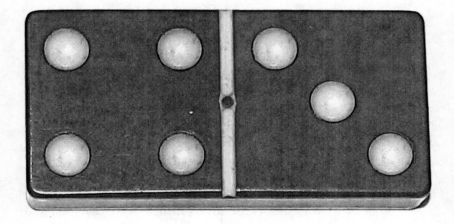

Key Word:

Authority

Additional meanings:

Control, confidence, stability, leadership, power

Numerological values:

3, 4, 7

4 / 3

You have power and authority but you must learn to stand up and exert what you have, not only for your own sake but for others also. Although you may sometimes be reluctant to use what power and authority you possess, you must not hesitate to do so when it is called for. You can be powerful and authoritative with love; you do not have to rule with an iron fist.

You can be the defender of the weak. Others may turn to you, either specifically asking for your help or merely implying that they could use it. Be ready to help at any time. Draw on your connections, if necessary. Speak with others in authority. Work as a diplomat when needed. At the same time, don't let your time be taken up with minor, petty problems. You can deal with the more important troubles but don't hesitate to delegate others — those you can trust — to work on your behalf.

There may be forces that are working against you, whether or not you are aware of them. You are well able to take care of them and to defeat them.

There may come about a sudden change — quite unexpected — that will bring a major shift in your life. You are used to thinking in a certain way and following a predictable pattern, but be prepared for all of this to change. You will have to compromise some of your long-held beliefs and modify some of your opinions. This will lead to a more aggressive attitude. There may be a change in diet called for. You will no longer be content to sit back and let things happen as they may, but will become an active part of what's happening; making many of the changes that take place around you.

4 / 4

Key Word:

Ritualism

Additional meanings:

Inspiration, appreciation of heritage, mercy. Beware tendency toward the unorthodox.

Numerological values:

4, 8

4 / 4

*T*his tile indicates that this is a good time for the creation of a partnership of some sort; a coming together of two or more individuals or groups. They will work well together and bring great success — greater than could be achieved by any one working independently. This could equally indicate a marriage or other love relationship. Certainly the partnership — whatever its form — should have strong male and female energies of near equal proportions.

This is a time to expand horizons and to explore new paths. Old habits need to be broken. This is a good time to enroll for courses, classes, instruction of all sorts; a good time to learn a foreign language.

There is also a spiritual spark ignited, with an attraction to religion in some form. There may be contact with your Higher Self and a breakthrough of some sort in or through meditation. You will achieve a greater sense of well-being and feel more accepting of what you had previously seen as your own short-comings.

This tile also indicates the presence of a gift. It may be something which you receive unexpectedly or it may be a gift which you give. Both the giving and the receipt of the gift will be a rewarding experience, bringing happiness and satisfaction.

4 / 5

Key Word:

Attraction

Additional meanings:

Harmony, love, deep feelings.
Beware any tendency toward quarreling, fickleness.

Numerological values:

4, 5, 9

4 / 5

*T*here is a strong attraction to another person. This person would make you feel more complete insofar as most of their thoughts, views, lifestyle, etc, are almost directly the opposite of your own. Although opposite, they are not antagonistic but merely complete and complement what is missing in your own outlook on life. The two of you would make one perfect whole. This may be a romantic attraction or it could be one of business, sporting activities, or similar. It may not be a single person but a group of people, as in becoming an essential part of a team.

The attraction might also be on a spiritual level, with a sense of completeness or wholeness recognized. The attraction may be to a particular discipline or education; perhaps to a religious philosophy.

This is a tile that frequently deals with your career; your vocation. These are important at this time. Consider how you relate to others and to your immediate community. How are you seen by them? What sort of an image do you project? It would be well worth your while to take some time to review these two questions and to acknowledge that you don't always show yourself the way that you would like to be perceived. Perhaps it's your physical appearance, or your speech and speech patterns. Do you always think before you speak or are you inclined to blurt out whatever comes into your head? This could be a good time to look over these aspects of yourself and your presentation to others.

Many times when this tile is drawn you find yourself becoming extremely busy in your dealings with other people. If this should be the case, bear in mind what has been said about your presentation and how you are perceived by others.

4 / 6

Key Word:

Accomplishment

Additional meanings:

Triumph, conquest, financial triumph.
Beware tendency toward unethical victory.

Numerological values:

1, 4, 6, 10

4 / 6

This is a tile of trust — trust in yourself. This means total trust. Follow your heart and your deeper inclinations and you will accomplish great things. Any battles you are to fight right now are with yourself and with having faith in your own judgement. There is discrimination necessary here; the ability to dig down to the main source and to discard all extraneous material.

Patience enters into this tile. It can take time to learn to trust, even to trust yourself. And when you have arrived at a decision, it can sometimes take time for the effects of your resulting actions to be seen. You may become frustrated, wanting to act quickly and not taking the time to think things through as thoroughly as you should. Fight that frustration and impatience. Discipline yourself to follow the path you know to be right, which is the path of reasoning, patience, and firm action.

This is a tile of victory; a just victory. If the law is involved, then justice will be served. The truth will be brought out. If there is competition involved, then you will triumph. There is the possibility of a challenge of some sort being issued to you. If so, have every confidence in yourself, act ethically, and you will triumph.

There is also the possibility of an accident, but it is one that will not be serious and from which you will recover completely.

5 / 0

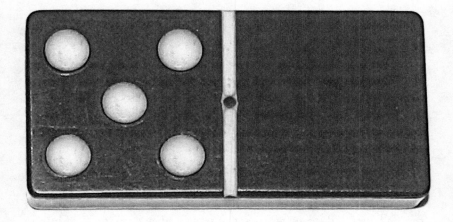

Key Word:

Determination

Additional meanings:

Energy, resolution, conquest.
Beware tendency toward lack of faith.

Numerological values:

5

5/0

Changes can come suddenly and unexpectedly. You need determination to deal with some of the challenges that may arise. This tile shows that you have determination. However, you may need time and discipline to build-up that resolution. Don't lose faith in yourself. Know that you do have the inner ability to face up to virtually any challenge and to stare it down. You need to get rid of anything that would weaken your determination. It is good to have scruples. A scruple is *"a sense of moral responsibility making one reluctant or unwilling to do wrong."*[1] Always keep that in mind; to do no wrong.

You have incredible courage to confront any obstacles at this time. You are well able to call upon your inner, and outer, personal strength to deal with any opposition that may arise, threatening to hinder or delay your forward motion through life. There is a cycle at work here. As you deal with opposition, so you build-up your confidence to handle any and all situations. And as you develop your self-confidence, you are better able to successfully meet the challenges.

There are also new beginnings with this tile. What has gone before has outgrown its usefulness and it's now time to regroup, reorganize, and move forcefully in a new direction. There's no need to spend time mourning what has gone before, for that has all been a step toward this new path. Everything is experience toward the future. This tile can signify a cycle of self-transformation and a rite of passage.

••••••••••••••••••••••••
1   *Chambers 21st Century Dictionary*

5 / 1

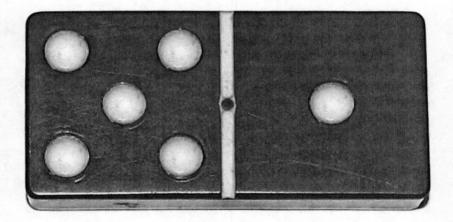

Key Word:

Counsel

Additional meanings:

Knowledge, withdrawal, search for truth, possible journey

Numerological values:

1, 5, 6

5 / 1

*T*his is a tile of completeness in that there is a feeling of having achieved a personal spiritual goal. There is indication of an inner understanding and mastery of personal consciousness.

This tile indicates a need for a period of time to be spent in solitude or meditation, to develop your inner skills and talents. You have great psychic perception when you apply yourself. You can be intuitive and in tune with the consciousness of others. However, this takes application and practice. The inner journeying of the shaman, the *"vision quest"* of the Native American, are two examples of the type of introspection and psychic awareness and development you need at this time. If you don't already, develop a daily regimen of meditation. It might also be beneficial to take an actual physical journey, going to where you can be completely alone in surroundings totally foreign to you.

It may be that you are already in the process of going through this period of self-examination. Don't expect it to go quickly; this can be a prolonged development and self-improvement. It does, however, bode well in that you will see rewards for work done and will recognize how you have advanced from where you were a month or two before.

If you have been working on what has been a long-term project, look for its completion — successful completion — in the very near future. Where you have been wondering if the effort was worth it, you will find that it most certainly was and you will enjoy the profits for a long time to come. There was no quick process to bring about this result. It was going to take time whatever the approach, so know that nothing has been wasted.

5 / 2

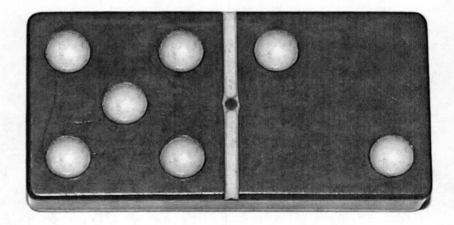

Key Word:

Opportunity

Additional meanings:

*Change, unexpected good fortune, success.
Beware setbacks, outside influences.*

Numerological values:

2, 5, 7

5/2

*T*his tile shows that there can be a complete change of attitude; an about-face on many issues. It's as though a bell, or a light bulb, has gone off inside your head and you have had a sudden revelation. This has occurred at just the right moment for change to be made and to be its most effective. This is no time to listen to the thoughts of others concerning your actions.

Have faith in yourself and your decisions, and act. There is a sudden opportunity that is not to be missed. By seizing it, you will not only gain an immediate reward but you will change the course of your life for the better. It will be natural for you to have a moment of doubt. You may feel that you are flying in the face of reason and taking a tremendous risk, but be firm in your inner faith.

This tile is the end of one cycle and the beginning of another. It is the start of what will turn out to be a long and eventful journey; one leading to success and good fortune. There will be many experiences along the way, all of which will be enlightening and revealing. You will emerge from what, by comparison, would seem to have been the fog of advancement into the bright light of evolution and attainment.

Your eyes are opened to a new and positive outlook on life, with all things in balance and harmony, and with success at your feet.

5 / 3

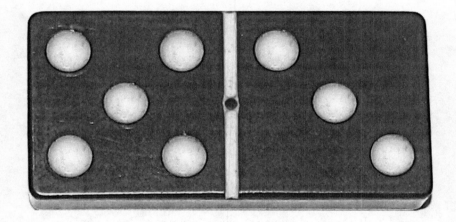

Key Word:

Balance

Additional meanings:

Fairness, harmony, equality, rightness.

Numerological values:

3, 5, 8

5 / 3

This tile ties-in with thoughts of close friends and family, as you might think of them when together celebrating festivals or events. These are times when small differences are forgotten and transgressions, real or imagined, are forgiven. There is a warmth and generosity that generates love and friendship.

Family and close friends are important to you at this time. Relationships, connections, shared interests; these are all crucial to you right now. There may be connections with social groups and community events, which bring pleasure and contentment.

There is fairness and justice surrounding this tile. It's immaterial what you think is fair and just; here the majority rules, perhaps in the guise of the federal authorities. Be prepared to reap what you have sown, so if you have nothing with which to reproach yourself then you have nothing to fear. Should you have any legal question awaiting an answer, then know that the ruling will be just, whether or not it favors yourself.

From knowledge comes understanding. You are now beginning to understand what had previously seemed perplexing to you. Knowledge had come to you before but you had not sufficiently digested it; to make the necessary association. Now all becomes clear and you are in a position to celebrate. You have new clarity and new energy. You feel like a new person. This is a good time to review all of your plans for your future, and to revise, amend, or cancel as you now see fit. You now feel better aligned to go forward to what you can see as a successful future.

5 / 4

Key Word:

Suspense

Additional meanings:

Apathy, interruption, intolerance. Beware wasted effort, possible arrogance, and false prophecy

Numerological values:

4, 5, 9

5/4

*B*etween death and rebirth there lies a period — usually short — that is idle, infertile and barren. Such is the period existing at the moment. It presages a new direction; new action and excitement. But for now, it is only suspenseful. You have a sense of being totally powerless. You are adrift in a boat without a rudder; no control as to direction and no knowledge as to inclination.

What is in evidence at the moment is not necessarily the result of anything you have done. It is the result of circumstances; circumstances over which you have had no control. You should not, therefore, be worried or anxious as to the outcome, for you will have no control over that. All you can do is to surrender to the situation and, by so doing, you will be the eventual victor. Do not look for outside help for none is coming. But none is needed.

It's possible that some sort of sacrifice may be needed. You may have to give up something of the old in order to gain something better in the new. But what would be gained is far superior to that which was relinquished. Here the tile may be intimating material assets, spiritual possessions, emotional ties, finances, relationships, vocation or avocation. Relax and do not cling to the past, for that would make letting go and moving on much more difficult and greatly delay the transition.

5 / 5

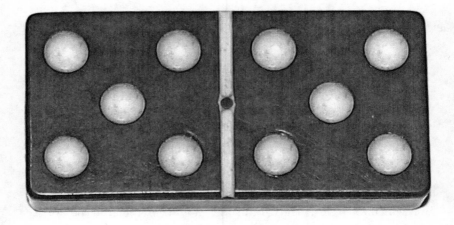

Key Word:
Transformation

Additional meanings:
Unexpected change, rebirth, occult interests

Numerological values:
1, 5, 10

5 / 5

This is the tile of endings and new beginnings. One demands the other: when one thing ends then another must begin, yet a new beginning can only occur after an ending.

This tile may signal the end of a relationship with an individual, a group, a job, a location — there are a great many possibilities. What is certain, however, is that although the relationship is ending, it is in order to open the way to a whole new relationship. The new one will be in many ways better and more satisfying than the old one.

This doesn't mean that there will be no remorse, no bad feelings, over the ending. You may well suffer mentally, emotionally, perhaps financially. But the fact remains that this is a catharsis; a cleansing that is opening the way to a far better situation.

Resulting from this change, or simply as an adjunct to it, you will develop a growing interest in matters metaphysical. Esoteric secrets, ancient mysteries, secret societies and similar will all begin to hold a fascination for you. You won't necessarily become involved in any of these but you will spend time investigating and evaluating them. You will become aware, or more aware, of your Higher Self and of spiritualism generally. Repeated patterns which you may have previously ignored, or attributed to *"coincidence,"* will now take on a special significance, frequently leading to in-depth investigation and evaluation. You will become more aware of psychic gifts, such as extra sensory perception, psychometry, and dream evaluation.

There could be a number of surprises in store for you, bringing with them unexpected gains, financial and otherwise.

5 / 6

Key Word:

Modification

Additional meanings:

Adaptation, coordination, harmony. Beware tendency toward separation, quarrelling.

Numerological values:

2, 5, 6, 11

5/6

*T*his tile indicates a need and realization that change would be good for you. You feel restricted in many ways and would enjoy more freedom. And change is on its way! It will be sudden and striking. Insofar as we create our own realities, it will not be entirely unexpected — on the unconscious level. However devastating it may seem on first appraisal, it will turn out to be releasing and transforming. This is not just a change of plans; it is a complete change of lifestyle.

Many times we experience an inner feeling that perhaps change is needed; that perhaps we should reconsider our situation and make some modifications and adjustments. This is not those feelings – this is major change, coming swiftly, unexpectedly, and in many cases devastatingly! But when it happens, you will feel in many ways refreshed. You will acknowledge that it is exactly what you needed, and you will make the necessary adjustments.

This will be a chance to completely clean house. Many changes are only partial so that, although major components are altered, you still retain some of the small things that you actually might have preferred to have thrown out. But this change is complete. It is wiping clean the slate and starting from scratch. Over the years you have developed (consciously or unconsciously) various pretensions, affectations, habits bad and good. These will be erased.

If you had been considering some plan of action in the near future, then put off making a final decision on it for a while. This major change needs to go through and it may well include changing your perspective on what you had in mind. Don't try to force issues, hoping to complete plans before this coming disruption. Instead, back off and relax. Patience is needed, and will be needed for a while.

6 / 0

Key Word:

Downfall

Additional meanings:

Malevolence, punishment, bondage. Beware tendency toward self-destruction; handicaps.

Numerological value:

6

6 / 0

*T*he tile indicates that you are trapped in your own reality. Your mental, emotional, and physical ideas are keeping you from expanding, developing, and creating. There is a sense of needing to punish yourself for some non-specific transgression(s). You may have thoughts of *"not being worthy"* or *"not deserving"*. In extreme cases there could be some form of self abuse.

A broken relationship may have triggered this condition. If so, let it go. It may have been personal, job-related, environmental, or other. Whatever brought about the break-up is not what's important here. What is important is your recovery from it. There needs to be a catharsis; a cleansing. Face-up to the situation, accept it as being part of life's experience, and let it go. There are endings in life and there are beginnings. The one brings about the other. Accept this as an ending but also as a new beginning.

There is the possibility that lies and untruths have played a part in bringing about this situation. There may have been double standards. You may have been unwilling to make personal sacrifices for the good of others. Determine that from now on you will do your utmost to always be honest and truthful, that you will do your best to help others when you are able, and that you will always try to see the other person's point of view. This does not imply weakness on your part. On the contrary, it calls for a great inner strength to act honorably and unemotionally in many situations in today's world. Draw on your inner strength, and learn to develop it.

It may be that you have lost a battle, or a decision of some sort, through the malevolence of another. There may have been a miscarriage of justice. You may have been punished or in some way restrained unjustly. Try not to hold a grudge. Try to forgive and forget and to move on in your life.

6 / 1

Key Word:

Sudden change

Additional meanings:

Breakdown of old beliefs, conflict.

Numerological values:

1, 6, 7

6 / 1

*T*his tile indicates that your psychic faculties are opening. You are becoming more and more aware of things which you *"pick up"* intuitively. You *"feel"* things before you actually see them or experience them. This may be something which you have not fully believed in before. Now, however, you are finding the proof of psychic abilities. Trust your feelings; go with what you feel is right.

Love often features in connection with this tile. There is a finding of love or an expansion of love. There may be a sudden realization that what you had been taking for granted, in terms of affection from another, is actually far more than that. You are blessed in that there is a close connection for you with another. Feelings are reciprocated; and they are deep. This connection — this attunement — may not be with an individual but with a group, an organization, an ideal, a vocation or avocation. There is, though, a sudden change in feelings and in appreciation.

In a sense, what you have experienced in life to this point is about to be destroyed. But this is not necessarily a bad thing. It is more of an awakening; an awareness that shows you, far more clearly than you have ever seen before, the path that lies ahead of you. You have been too close to the woods to see the trees. Now you are able to step back and view the whole scene and, consequently, appreciate the balance and the colors and complements that are there.

6 / 2

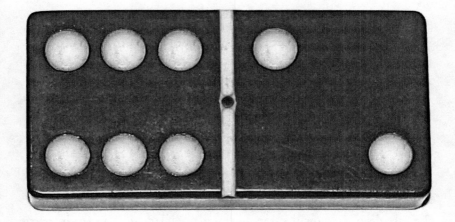

Key Word:

Inspiration

Additional meanings:

Improvement, insight, hope, faith,
spiritual love, enlightenment.
Beware tendency toward doubt, and pessimism

Numerological values:

2, 6, 8

6 / 2

*T*his tile is one confirming your inner strength. You have wonderful spiritual guidance, whether or not you are aware of it. On some level — perhaps the unconscious — you know that you have a great intelligence and have untapped abilities. This is a tile that indicates the brightness of your true nature. You have a wisdom that is ancient; possibly from many lifetimes of earthly experience.

Others look to you for guidance. You receive questions such as *"What do you think?"* *"What would you do?"* and similar. On the surface they seem like casual queries where the answers you give will not be taken seriously. Yet in fact what you say always does make a difference; the people asking do take note of what you say and invariably find your advice to be the best. With this in mind, you should never give glib answers to questions, no mater how frivolous those questions may seem to be. Always give deep thought to what is being asked and try to offer the best advice you can.

You can be the catalyst for change in others. By example, and by the giving of advice, you can make significant changes in people's lives. You could be a great diplomat, mediating different sides and opinions.

This tile is also associated with birth. It can denote a coming birth of life or of an idea or concept. It is the result of actions and ideas. It is a start. As a start, it means that things will proceed and that they will improve. There is a lot of positive energy in this tile. See it and use it as the jumping-off point for new ideas and directions, for new projects and new relationships.

6 / 3

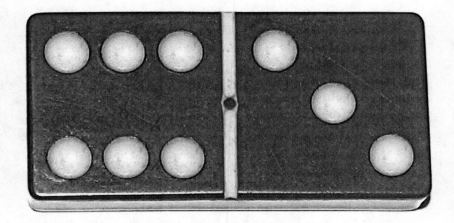

Key Word:

Deception

Additional meanings:

Warning, imagination, trickery, psychic powers. Possibility of unexpected gain.

Numerological values:

3, 6, 9

6 / 3

Whatever you see is not necessarily what you get. Proceed with caution. Be especially careful when dealing with psychic matters. Many times there are *"hidden agendas,"* or you may find that what looked innocent is actually a whole can of worms that you have inadvertently opened. There is the possibility of disappointment and disillusionment with a number of personal matters.

If there are decisions to be made, don't be too quick to arrive at them. Spend as long as is necessary checking and re-checking, especially where finances and figures are involved. Be careful of time frames and due dates or deadlines. There is the possibility of a miscarriage of justice resulting from false testimony. Look for — and demand — proof of statements, with documentary evidence if necessary. Your honor, or the honor of someone near and dear to you, may be involved here. That is something well worth fighting for, but don't be surprised to find that some fighting may be unfair and inappropriate.

Many problems can develop through unnecessary haste. They could be easily avoided if you took the time — plenty of time — to examine what is going on, who is involved, and the veracity of what is being presented. Don't be tempted to make a quick decision thinking that by doing so the whole mess will go away. It won't. It will only get worse. Force yourself to have patience and to examine the details.

Much of what has been said applies to you personally. Examine your own thoughts and feelings; your own motivations for wanting or doing things. Do you have a secret agenda? Are you trying to force someone else's hand? Examine your motives and enter the playing field knowing that you are as clean and virtuous as you can be. Only then can you fight with a clear conscience.

6 / 4

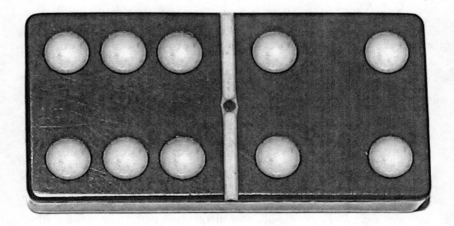

Key Word:
happiness

Additional meanings:

*Satisfaction, attainment, love, joy, contentment.
Beware tendency toward loneliness;
possibility of delayed success.*

Numerological values:
1, 4, 6, 10

6 / 4

*T*his is a tile of good health, achievement, and success in all things. There is here the culmination of all that you have worked for. You will enjoy love, joy, and satisfaction in knowing that you have brought all of this upon yourself through your own actions. Your plans have succeeded; you can celebrate victory.

There is great healing energy here. You could be a natural healer. If you have not already done so, become involved in some form of healing, be it hands-on, reiki, auric, spiritual, or whatever. You can bring a lot of benefits to others and, through them, to yourself.

There are gifts arriving or on the way. These may be tangible or they may be in the form of opportunities for you to take. This is a wonderful time for investing, both financially and also the investing of your time and energy into projects that give you happiness.

You may be aware of some part of yourself that you have long kept closed, for whatever reasons. Now is the time to open up every aspect of yourself. Open up and let in the light of knowledge and of being. Allow yourself to feel happy and content. Allow yourself to embrace the All-That-Is; the Life Force of the world. See the goodness in every aspect of Nature and relish the brotherhood and sisterhood that we all share.

6 / 5

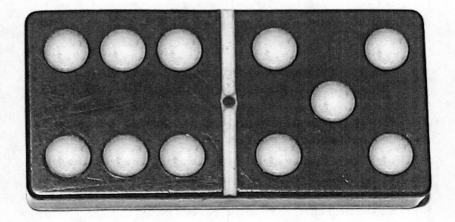

Key Word:
Renewal

Additional meanings:

*Rejuvenation, awakening, development, promotion.
Beware tendency toward self-doubt, self-judgement*

Numerological values:
2, 5, 6, 11

6 / 5

*T*his tile says that there may be hold-ups to what you desire. You need to consider, and reconsider, your plans. Go over the details and the possibilities. Look for reasons for delays and see whether or not they can be traced to you. In other words, are you erecting your own barriers to success? You may have deeply ingrained biases . . . even bigotry of one form or another. This could have come from your upbringing or from negative experiences of the past. Try to wipe clean the slate; to start afresh and with a positive attitude.

This is a time to pay-off old debts and to mend fences. Seek out those with whom you have disagreements and make a very real effort to find a compromise. You receive what you give, so give-out love and give it freely.

There is recognition here of emotional and spiritual need, with a further need for patience. You feel that some of your personal needs are not being met and that you are being forced to act, perhaps rashly. But there's time for contemplation of possible actions. Do not act hastily. There is nothing that cannot wait until you have thought through all of your dealings and what will be brought about by them.

Promotion in your job is possible. If not promotion, then increased responsibility. You will feel the pressure of this. But again, if you take the time to plan your actions and refuse to be rushed, you will succeed and succeed well.

6 / 6

Key Word:

Completion

Additional meanings:

*Attainment, new beginning, triumph, capability.
Beware tendency toward lack of vision,
refusal to learn.*

Numerological values:

3, 6, 12

6 / 6

*T*his tile indicates the acquaintance, and growing friendship, of an older male of influence. He is in a position of power and is financially stable. If not an individual, then this will be acquaintance with a situation or a business corporation of money and power, which can aid and influence your life. There may be a connection with banking or the law.

The indication could also be for connection and communication with your Higher Self or Guardian Angel. Such connection will bring a wonderful sense of exhilaration and awareness of all that you have accomplished. You will feel a sense of protection and experience the freedom to act without worrying about the consequences.

Your talents and abilities are recognized. Accept offers of help that may come at this time, for they will rapidly advance you along the path you have chosen. Learn to trust your intuition, especially when it comes to the acceptance of financial aid. You may have been looking for a patron of some sort, to back you in promoting ideas which you have had for some time. Review your plans and double-check your calculations. There is about to be an opportunity such as you have long dreamed about. Be ready when it comes.

You have had a thorough training in *"life."* You often feel that you have experienced most things; the good and the bad. Now is the time to put that training to good use. This will bring you a feeling of completeness; of having finally come full circle.

General Interpretations

*T*hese are the interpretations that have been used for generations for quick readings; leaning more toward the fortune-telling aspect rather than the in-depth insights given above. As I've said, there is nothing wrong with this approach and many times it can bring about a familiarity with the dominoes which then, later, leads to the more analytical approach.

Generally speaking, all Sixes are connected with good luck; Fives refer to jobs and careers; Fours deal with financial matters; Threes are connected to love; Twos refer to family and close friends; Ones indicate journeys to be taken. All blanks refer directly to the Querent.

Layout 1

Here is one way to give a very quick reading. The dominoes are spread out, face down, and thoroughly mixed. Up to three people may each draw three dominoes, which they place face-up in a line, horizontally, across in front of them. The tile on the left represents the past; that in the center, the present; and that on the right, the future. With just the broad meanings given above, a general reading can be given.

For example, if the drawn dominoes are: Two:Three, One:Five, and Four:Blank, then it could be said that in the past the Querent had a number of very close friends and family, with much love around. At present, there is some travel to be undertaken, connected with his or her employment. And in the future, there are going to be some financial matters that will affect the Querent personally.

Layout 2

Face down, mix the dominoes. Take from those closest to you for Present; from the middle of the pile for Near Future; and farthest from you for Future.

Layout 3

"Now and Then" or *"Present & Future"*. Draw one and one tiles; one and two; two and two; or two and three. No more than one drawing per session with sessions no more frequent than once a month.

There are more detailed meanings which need to be considered, however. These are shown in the *"doubles."*

Double Six:
The marriage of the Querent. If already married, then there will be good fortune coming as a result of that marriage.

Double Five:
A job promotion, to a better paid, higher position.

Double Four:
Unexpected money coming in a dramatic way.

Double Three:
The Querent will unexpectedly fall in love.

Double Two:
There will be new friends who will become close and dear.

Double One:
A wonderful, and very enjoyable, vacation journey is on its way.

Double Blank:
Extreme caution needs to be exercised. This is one domino that can be a serious warning.

Apart from these short meanings, there are longer interpretations possible which can be read from just one of the dominoes, as you'll see below. Many diviners will therefore have the Querent pick only one. (*Again, in this way, many people can pick a tile from the full deck at the same time.*) The upturned dominoes have the following traditional meanings, for this more in-depth divination:

Double Six:

A happy marriage, with children. Riches by speculation, so a good domino when considering the stock market. It also indicates a rise in land values.

Six:Five:

If you're looking for a job, this says that persevering will bring you to a good one. Similarly, if you're looking for love don't be discouraged by rebuffs; success awaits you. There is here luck in purchasing real estate but the possibility of being cheated buying jewelry, silverware, or a watch. If you're waiting on a possible inheritance, there's a good chance you will get it.

Six:Four:

Early marriage followed by much happiness. Children will be equally divided between boys and girls. When grown, they will all leave home early. Neither wealth nor poverty is indicated with this tile.

Six:Three:

A domino for constancy and affection. It shows an early marriage with much happiness and no troubles to mar it. There will also be honors and riches. There is a slight possibility of death in middle age but, if you survive that, you will live to a ripe old age.

Six:Two:

Excellent domino for lovers, foretelling a happy marriage. Those looking for luck in business will find more profits than they expected. However, if there are any dishonest schemes, they will be *"rewarded"* with disaster.

Six:One:

To young married people, this tile indicates that they will be better off in later life than they are now. To older people: that the later part of life was better than the earlier. It can also indicate that there will be a second marriage that will be better than the first.

Six:Blank:

This tile is an indicator of death to someone near to you, be it a close friend or an acquaintance. It may also indicate the death of an animal.

Double Five:

This is lucky in all ways: finances, job, marriage. It does not mean you will become rich, but it does signify good luck.

Five:Four:

This is not a good tile where money is concerned. If you have money, you may lose it or you may find that you owe more than you realized.

Five:Three:

You will never be poor, but you may never be rich. You will always have sufficient. If you already have money, you will not gain much more. It indicates much the same where love and sex is concerned — status quo.

Five:Two:

This is a reasonably fair card for women but not so for men. If in love, or married, the woman may turn out to have a short temper. A marriage may turn out to appear happy and successful on the outside but will deteriorate and be unhappy in the end. Financial speculation will not be successful.

Five:One:

For those fond of excitement, this is a good tile. There is the possibility of an invitation to an event that will thrill you. If money is expected, there will be disappointment. A young woman may find an admirer who is rich but rough. She will discard him and marry another.

Five:Blank:

To a man, this tile implies that there is a certain amount of dishonesty present, with a tendency to gambling or sex. To a woman, this indicates an unhappy love affair.

Double Four:

A good, smooth sign for lovers, for farmers, and all laborers. But for professional people this indicates hard times to come. There is also a wedding in the near future.

Four:Three:

Those who turn this tile will marry young, live happily, and will not have more than one child. There is neither poverty nor riches here. Married persons who have children already will face the possibility of a long separation and even a second marriage.

Four:Two:

There will be a change in your circumstances, which could be for the better or for the worse. It may be something slight or something that will be very traumatic. If you have offended anyone dear to you, this tile shows that you will soon make up with them.

Four:One:

Referring to married couples, the more children in the marriage, the more the financial position will deteriorate. Those who are unmarried may soon get married, with the same results. If there are no children, the bank account will grow.

Four:Blank:

This is an unfortunate tile for lovers. It foretells arguments and quarrels; possibly separations. If you should trust a friend with a secret, the secret will not be kept. There is also an indication, with this tile, that your partner is a believer in the occult.

Double Three:

Nothing to do with love or matrimony but does indicate the accumulation of riches. There is no indication of any unhappiness associated with the buildup of wealth.

Three:Two:

This is a good tile for the following: love-making, marriage, recovery of stolen property, travel, speculation, collecting on a debt, planting a crop. It is, however, a bad tile for gamblers.

Three:One:

A young woman turning this tile will be likely to lose her virginity. A married woman will be approached by a man with a view to having an affair. For a man, this foretells the loss of money through illicit sex. It is not a favorable domino for anyone.

Three:Blank:

Your sweetheart is artful and deceitful. If you are married, the wife will be shrewish and vain; the husband will be dull, slow, and not very bright. This tile may also indicate that you will be invited to a party where you will be attracted to someone, but it will end with a violent quarrel.

Double Two:

Success in love matters and much happiness. Success in any undertaking. No great riches but there will be comfort.

Two: One:

A woman will marry young and her husband will die young, leaving her wealth and property. She will later remarry. A man will have a life of luxury, will never marry, but will be a favorite of the ladies. Not a good tile for business people, since it foretells losses by failures.

Two:Blank:

Poverty and bad luck. This is a tile of good luck for thieves and dishonest people, indicating success in shady dealings. In reference to any possible journey, it indicates a safe passage.

Double One:

Affectionate constancy and happiness in the married state. This is an excellent tile to turn, both for lovers and for married people.

Double Blank:

The worst tile of the whole set. Bad luck to everyone except the dishonest and unscrupulous, for whom it means rewards. Unfavorable for love and for business.

One way to give a quick reading is to mix the dominoes face down and then take from those closest to you for the Present; from the middle for the Near Future; and from the farthest for the Future. An alternate would be *"Now and Then"* or *"Present & Future"* — drawing just two tiles. In these instances, there should be no more than one drawing per session with sessions no more frequent than once a month.

Another method is for the dominoes to be thoroughly mixed, face down. Up to three people may then each draw three dominoes, which they place face up in a line, horizontally, across in front of them. The tile on the left represents the past; that in the center, the present; and that on the right, the future.

As stated previously, it may be easier to have all the dominoes in a bag and to simply shake them and then reach in and take however many are required.

Dömínöes / Tarot Equivalency

One way of giving a detailed reading of the dominoes is by equating each tile with one of the tarot cards. In this way, as you turn a domino face-up you connect it to a tarot card and then *"read"* as though you had that card, rather than the tile, in front of you (this presumes a knowledge of the tarot cards so that you can *"see,"* in your mind's eye, a specific card).

There are 78 tarot cards in a deck but only 28 dominoes (with 49 possible arrangements of the tiles). We therefore work with the 8, 9, 10, Page, Knight, Queen, King of the Minor Arcana and the whole of the Major Arcana. All dominoes are laid down horizontally.

	Left Side		Right Side
0	Cups	0 = 8	
1	Wands	1 = 9	
2	Swords	2 = 10	
3	Pentacles	3 = Page	
4, 5, 6	Major Arcana	4 = Knight	
		5 = Queen	
		6 = King	

In other words, a domino showing a 0 on the left (as mentioned, they are always laid down horizontally) is always of the Cups suit; a 1 on the left is of the Wands; 2 is Swords, and 3 is Pentacles. The number on the right indicates the card in that suit, with 0 being 8; 1 being 9; 2 being 10; 3 being Page; 4 being Knight; 5 being Queen, and 6 being King. [It will be seen that there is no 0 : 0 equivalent here, and therefore no Eight of Cups. The 0 : 0 is reserved for The Fool in the Major Arcana *(see below)*]:-

Cups	Wands	Swords	Pentacles	
	1 : 0	2 : 0	3 : 0	8
0 : 1	1 : 1	2 : 1	3 : 1	9
0 : 2	1 : 2	2 : 2	3 : 2	10
0 : 3	1 : 3	2 : 3	3 : 3	Page
0 : 4	1 : 4	2 : 4	3 : 4	Knight
0 : 5	1 : 5	2 : 5	3 : 5	Queen
0 : 6	1 : 6	2 : 6	3 : 6	King

The Major Arcana is designated by dominoes that have 4, 5 or 6 on the left:-

Major Arcana

4 : 0	Magician	5 : 0	Strength	6 : 0	Devil
4 : 1	High Priestess	5 : 1	Hermit	6 : 1	Tower
4 : 2	Empress	5 : 2	Wheel of Fortune	6 : 2	Star
4 : 3	Emperor	5 : 3	Justice	6 : 3	Moon
4 : 4	Hierophant	5 : 4	Hanged Man	6 : 4	Sun
4 : 5	Lovers	5 : 5	Death	6 : 5	Judgement
4 : 6	Chariot	5 : 6	Temperance	6 : 6	World
		0 : 0	Fool		

Here are some examples of the meaning of particular dominoes, following the above equivalencies, and showing the difference resulting from the lie of the tile:-

Examples:

2 : 3 = Page of Swords		3 : 2 = Ten of Pentacles
5 : 3 = Justice		3 : 5 = Queen of Pentacles
0 : 5 = Queen of Cups		5 : 0 = Strength

Layouts for Reading

*R*eading dominoes like tarot cards, they may be laid out in much the same way that the cards are. As, for example, in the Celtic Cross method, the Astrological Spread, or any of the popular spreads. Most books on the tarot contain several suggested patterns for laying down the cards. These can all be followed, but laying down the dominoes instead of cards.

Celtic Cross Layout

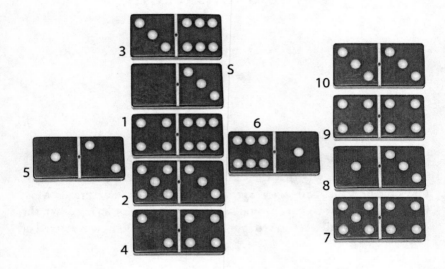

	3 = Above		
5 = Behind	S = Significator;	6 = Ahead	10 = Final Outcome
	1 = What *"covers"*		9 = Hopes & Fears
	2 = What *"crosses"*		8 = House
	4 = Beneath		7 = Self

Astrological Circle

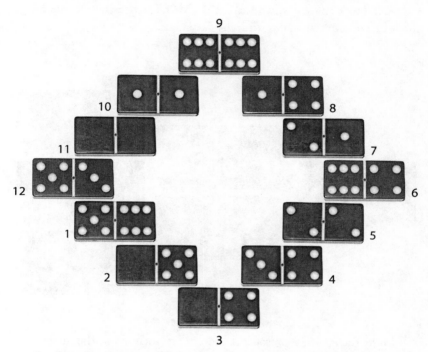

In this, the positions of the dominoes represent the Houses and are interpreted according to the House meanings.

For example:

First House represents the personality and outer appearance.

Second House: money and possessions.

Third House: relationships, education and communications.

Fourth House: parents, the home, start and end of life.

Fifth House: creativity, children, enterprises.

Sixth House: service, work.

Seventh House: marriage, close relationships.

Eighth House: death, money from legacies.

Ninth House: travel, further education, foreigners.

Tenth House: careers, ambitions, social status.

Eleventh House: friendship, societies.

Twelfth House: confinement, escapism, service.

Trumpet Layout

A layout I enjoy is what I call TRUMPET, since there is the rough shape of a megaphone, or Spiritualist Trumpet:

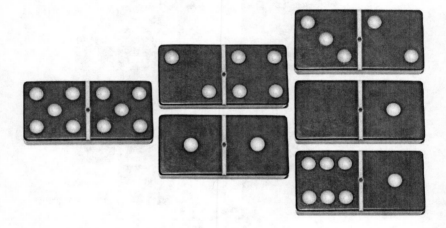

Here, the far left represents the forces presently about the subject; the center two represent the forces coming into play in the near future; and the last three show the forces that are forming in the far future.[2]

In this example, there is the equivalent of the tarot cards' *"Death"* (transformation) card on the left (present); Knight of Swords and Nine of Wands in the center (near future); and Ten of Pentacles, Nine of Cups, and Tower cards on the right (far future).

●●●●●●●●●●●●●●●●●●●●●●●●●
2.　　　*Always bear in mind that, for all forms of divination, it is not possible to see more than about twelve months ahead. Any term "Future" or "Final Outcome" should always be considered with this in mind.*

Numerological Significance

*A*nother ingredient that may be brought into the equation, when reading dominoes, is the numerological significance. If there is an individual connected with the tile, then this number can give a good picture of the person concerned (the significance can also be applied to a group of people or a situation).

The two sides of the domino must first be considered separately. This is somewhat like looking at both the Sun Sign and the Moon Sign in astrology. The two can then be added together, reduced to a single digit if necessary (*see below*), and then also considered as that number. Again to equate to astrology, this resultant can be like looking at the Rising Sign or Ascendent.

The number gives general information as well as that pertaining to specific persons.

In numerology, the numerals 1 through 9 give the basis of all numbers and calculations. Pythagorus said *"The world is built upon the power of numbers."* He was the one who reduced all to the power of the nine primaries. This is done by adding anything above 9.

For example:

$$26 = 2 + 6 = 8.$$

No matter the size of the number, it can be reduced in the same way.

eg: 7,548,327 would become:

$$7 + 5 + 4 + 8 + 3 + 2 + 7 = 36 = 3 + 6 = 9.$$

Number Values

The following values are attached to the nine primary numbers, as they delineate people and things:

1:
SUN
Element: Fire;
Colors: Orange, Gold, Yellow, Bronze;
Weekday: Sunday

Number One is known as *"the All."* It is the omnipotent; the deity; the symbol of light. A single dot on the domino symbolizes the Life Force itself; the beginning of all things. If the domino is associated with a person, then that person is very much the extrovert and is a leader and driving force who automatically assumes control and has lots of ambition. Such people have a tendency to be impatient and there are usually strong feelings, either for or against; seldom in the middle. This person often plays the role of *"Big Brother or Sister,"* to others and does not realize their own strength – yet would not knowingly hurt another. A Number One personality can stand praise, which may spur them on to further achievements.

2:
MOON
Element: Water;
Colors: Green (all shades), Cream;
Weekday: Monday

Two is the number of unity; is a joint force. Two has a great pacifying effect, giving balance and peace. Number Two people can be emotional and easily influenced to tears. Sensitive and domestic, they are very fond of the home but can easily accept changes in surroundings. A Two Personality has a fertile imagination, is patriotic, and has a preference for living near water. May have musical talents and great psychic ability.

3:
JUPITER
Element: Fire;
Colors: Red, Mauve, Blue;
Weekday: Thursday

Three is the number of activity, especially of physical activity. It is also a number of caution – or should be! Number Three people are interested in the material rather than the spiritual. This is the number of the scientist and investigator; the seeker; the ones wanting to know "*how*" and "*why.*" These people possess a very good sense of humor, and are not greatly interested in money. Religious ideas are flexible and they can be very trusting.

4:
URANUS
Element: Air;
Colors: Electric Blue, Grey;
Weekday: Sunday

Four is the number of the mind; typically working on analyzing and planning. However, being of the air element, many times Four can indicate amazing things which somehow get separated and lost, like straws blown away in the wind. This number indicates strong, intuitive tendencies. Dominoes connecting a Four to a person or people, show them as being very interested in the occult and in psychic research. They are usually ahead of their time and, because of this, often regarded as strange or eccentric. Four People are drawn to anything out of the ordinary. They believe in liberty and equality but can be bitingly sarcastic if crossed. They can be very good at predicting things.

5:
MERCURY
Element Air;
Colors: Indigo, Light Grey;
Weekday: Wednesday

Five is associated with hopes and aspirations; with good judgement and understanding; also activity, both physical and mental. There can be a religious connection and an underlying sympathy for the underdog. Five has hidden depths which contain many secrets. It can lead to a number of complications. Number Five people are fond of reading and research; are inquiring and exploring. They make friends easily, are good at languages and at simplifying systems. A Five personality can make a good teacher or writer, and is usually methodical and orderly.

6:
VENUS
Element: Earth;
Colors: Yellow, Pink, Rose;
Weekday: Friday

Six on a domino is a *"fortunate"* number that is frequently associated with happiness, in whatever form that may take. It is also associated with love. Number Six people are usually good looking. They are gentle and refined, pleasant and sociable, friendly and agreeable. A Number Six person is a natural peacemaker who is able to soothe ruffled feelings and would make an excellent diplomat. Number Six people are also excellent as hosts or hostesses, but can experience difficulties with finances.

7:
NEPTUNE
Element: Water;
Colors: Light Blue, Green, Yellow, White;
Weekday: Monday

The number Seven is associated with completion and finality but also with boredom and depression. It's also associated with intuition and spiritual aspirations. Number Seven people are extremely psychic, usually possessing E.S.P. They are frequently introverts who, although not saying much, think and know a great deal. These people can appear mysterious and are often interested in botany, chemistry, psychology and psychiatry. They may be knowledgeable in astrology and most occult fields. A Number Seven personality may enjoy fishing, and tend to take from the *"Haves"* to give to the *"Have Nots."*

8:
SATURN
Element: Earth;
Colors: Silver, Dark Grey, Dark Blue;
Weekday: Saturday

This is a number that is frequently coupled with ruthlessness and aggression. Destruction is often in or near the Eight. Eight People have little sense of humor, and are inclining to be cold and pessimistic. They believe that hard work never killed anyone. Although frequently slow off the mark, Number Eight people usually end up ahead of everyone else. They can be good at finances and are frequently connected with real estate, mining, and the law. They are often prepossessed with thoughts of the past and may be interested in cemeteries and pawn shops.

9:
MARS
Element: Fire;
Colors: Violet, Crimson, Rose;
Weekday: Tuesday

Nine is a symbol of nobility and compassion. It is also often associated with alienation and withdrawal. Number Nine people can be very jealous and get overly emotional. They may be active but frequently ruled by their emotions. Number Nine personalities can be tied to family background and are extremely loyal. They can be impulsive and afraid of the unknown, and are often associated with surgery and with illnesses, both physical and mental.

0:
PLUTO
Color: White

This is the sign of infinity and eternity. There is an explosive quality here. It is also a number of transformation; it is an ending but also a new beginning. Far from representing *"nothingness"*, it represents everything.

From the above it's possible to look at anyone from the Numerology point of view, based on the domino drawn.

Dominoes can be a wonderful, refreshing method of telling fortunes, or divining. These days, when so many people seem wed to the tarot cards, it makes a nice change to be able to offer a different system with a more unusual focus. As has been shown, the dominoes can serve as an alternative for the tarot and for the runes, but give some extra information through numerology and through pure intuitive feeling. As with all types of psychic work, it is constant practice that brings out the power we all have within us. Work with the dominoes and extend your abilities. Most of all, though — enjoy yourself!

Raymond Buckland

The Games of Dömïnöes

Dominoes are best known as a game for amusement. They have been so used for centuries. However, the *"Domino Diviner"* will find that playing the game is more than just amusement. By playing with the tiles, or *"bones"*[3], you really get the feel of them; they become almost alive! Many people have been drawn into doing divination with dominoes just as a natural follow-on to playing the games.

There are different games, and many variations, but the simplest and perhaps best known are the *"Block & Draw"* games. These may be played by two or more people.

The tiles are laid face down and well mixed. Before starting, the person who will begin — or who *"sets"* — is chosen by both players each drawing one tile at random. The one with the most dots on it is the winner. These two tiles are then returned to the set and mixed in. Any double beats single dots. For example, a 3:3 would beat a 5:6. (One variant is that there is only a winner if a double is drawn, with the highest double being that winner. If no doubles are drawn then the dominoes are returned to the pile and there is a new draw.)

Each player draws seven tiles. These are placed on edge, with the dots visible to the player but not to the opponent. Beginning with the one who sets, the tiles are placed one at a time, alternately by each player, face up on the table. Each player must match the end of the domino just played, proceeding lengthwise. In other words, if the first player plays a 2:3 the second player can match either the 2 end or the 3 end of that tile. In this manner you might make a line of tiles: 1:0 – 0:2 – 2:3 – 3:6 – 6:4. If you

••••••••••••••••••••••
3   *Some refer to the dominoes as "bones" and the ones left unplayed as "the boneyard".*

have a double, then it's placed cross-wise and following moves can go off from either end of that tile, or from the middle of it. Some rules say that if you play a double then you may take another turn, if you have a tile that matches it. *(e.g. you could play a 5:5 followed by a 5:3)*

If one player is blocked — i.e. cannot match the end of the previously-played tile — then he or she may pick up another tile from the *"boneyard"* and can, in fact, keep taking up new ones until there is a match. (Another *set of rules says that the player who cannot match shouts "Go!" to indicate that the opponent should continue.*

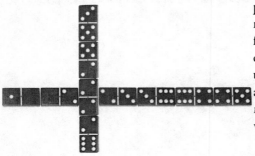

The opponent may then go on to lay down another tile, and can continue until eventually the other player can match one.)

The game ends when one player runs out of tiles, shouting *"Domino!"* Or the game can end when both players are blocked and unable to continue. If neither player can match, the player with the fewest dots in hand wins, and scores as many points as there are on the tiles of the loser. If both have the same number of tiles left, then the one with the fewer dots wins.

Keeping score, each player's score is the total number of dots on the opponent's remaining dominoes. A game may be for a total of 50 or for 100 points. Since the object is to be left with as few dots on the tiles as possible, the best ploy is to play your highest tile first, and always try to play high tiles. (*There can be a certain consolation to losing when the winner looks expectantly at your remaining tile, to see how many points he or she has won, and you turn it over to show it's a double zero!)*

There are many different forms of dominoes and many different games, including such names as *"42"*, *"Muggins"* (or *"All Five"*), *"All Threes"*, *"Flower & Scorpion"*, *"Sniff"*, *"Domino Whist"*, *"Bergen"*, *"Trains"*, *"Longana"*, and such Oriental games as *"Pai Gow"*, *"Tien Gow"*, *Tiu U"*, and *"Kap Tai Shap"*. There are also more difficult games for advanced players, such as *"Matador"*, *"Sebastopol"*, *"Cyprus"*, and *"Maltese Cross"*. Various games of solitaire can also be played with dominoes. Some of these games I detail below.

The skinny line of dominoes make some people think of a dragon, and hence the remainder pile of bones is the boneyard; either thought of as the skeleton of a dragon or the bones of its prey!

Blind Hughie
(or Blind Dominoes)

This game can be played with two, three or four players. As usual, each turns over a tile to determine who shall start, and the game proceeds clockwise. The tiles are then turned back to the face-down position and mixed.

Each player takes a number of dominoes and lays them in a line in front of him or her, face down. With two players, each takes eight tiles; with three players, each takes seven tiles; with four players, each takes six tiles.

Player #1 turns up any one of those in front, and places it in the center. Player #2 (going clockwise around) then turns up any tile. If there is a match with either end of Player #1's tile, then it is laid down in the usual manner. If there is no match, then Player #2 turns it back face down and places it at the right end of his or her dominoes.

Play follows around, with each turning face-up one tile and seeing whether or not it can be played. If it can't, then it's turned face-down and put at the right end of the player's line. There can be an advantage here if you can remember who has what, face down at the ends of their lines!

The winner is the first player to use all of his or her dominoes. Points are counted in the usual way: the winner scores the total number of dots on the remaining dominoes of the other players. Since not all 28 tiles are used, the game doesn't always end with one person using all of his or her tiles. Count the points in the usual way.

Hungarian Dominoes

This game can be played with two, three or four players. As usual, each turns over a tile to determine who shall start, and the game proceeds clockwise. The tiles are then turned back to the face-down position and mixed. With two players, each takes twelve tiles; with three players, each takes eight tiles; with four players, each takes six tiles.

As in Block Dominoes, each player puts his or her tiles on edge in front, to see what play is possible. The first player lays down a tile and then immediately follows it with whatever other tiles match, until unable to continue. The next player then continues and, again, lays down as many as possible. So on, around the circle. When no one can add any more tiles, the game ends and each player counts his or her remaining pips. The loser is the first person to reach 100 points, with the winner the one with the lowest score.

Cross Dominoes

This game can be played with four players. The tiles are in the face-down position and mixed. With the four players, each takes six tiles. As usual, the game proceeds clockwise.

The game starts with the highest double being played, and set crosswise. That starting player may then add another tile, or may pass. The others follow on, as usual, but having to add on to that first double. They must pass if unable to add a tile to any of the four possible ends.

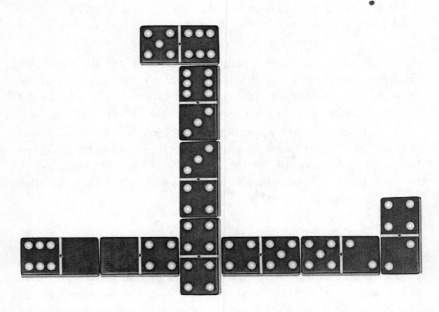

In the above example, the first tile was the 4:4. One player added the 4:0, another the 4:3 and another the 4:5. The fourth player wasn't able to add on (not having a 4 tile). This, then, left only three available ends for the continuing play: 0, 3, and 5. Because this bottom end of the first tile could not be played right away, it cannot be used by any succeeding players.

Variations: One set of rules says that if a player cannot play then he or she may draw from the boneyard. Another set of rules says there is no drawing from the boneyard; if you cannot play then you must pass.

Sebastopol

This game can be played with four players, each getting seven tiles. The game starts with the one holding the 6:6 setting that tile in the center of the table. The next player (*going clockwise*) must place another tile in the sixes suit against the 6:6. All of the other players must follow suit, each placing a 6 tile. If unable to add a 6 then that player passes. Once the four arms of 6 are taken care of, then the game continues with the arms growing on outward, with other doubles being placed end to end (*not across*). When one player shouts *"Domino!"* and wins, that player gets the total number of pips in the hands of the other players as his or her score. If the game blocks (*cannot continue*), then the player with the lowest score wins. He or she takes the total of the other players' pips and deducts the total of his or her own pips.

The game is played to a total of 60 or 100, as agreed between the players before starting.

Solitaire:
Castle Rock

All tiles are placed face down and shuffled. Draw three tiles and turn them face-up, placing them side by side. If the first and third tiles have a matching pip then the middle tile is removed and put to one side, back in the boneyard. If there is no match, then a new tile is taken from the boneyard and placed on the right of the other three. Again, if there is a match of pips on the two outer ones then the middle one is removed.

In the below example, there was no match with the first three so the fourth,

5:2, was added. The 5s matched so the 4:2 could be removed and returned to the boneyard. Another tile would then be added on the right. Again, if there was a match in the two outer tiles then the middle one could be removed. If all three tiles have a common number, then all three may be removed.

Whenever a tile is surrounded by tiles with a common number, the middle tile is removed.

The goal is to remove all the tiles from the set in order to win.

Solitaire:
Concentration

This game is basically a memory test. All 28 dominoes are placed face down. They are then turned over, in twos, to find matches. A match is a pair of tiles that total 12 points. This could be made up of (*for instance*) a 2:3 and a 3:4, or a 6:5 and a 0:1. If the two you turn over are a match then they should be removed. If they're not a match, then turn them back face-down. (*This is where it helps to remember what is where!*). Your score is the number of attempts it takes to clear the set. Try to better yourself each time.

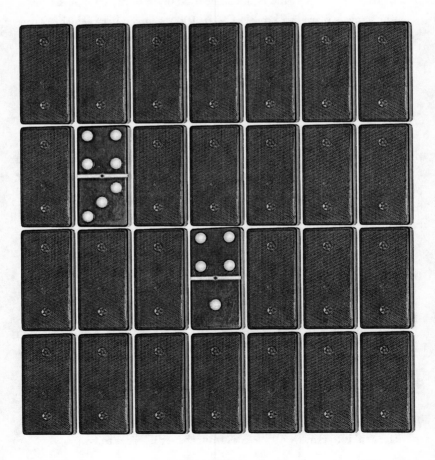

Recommended Reading

Adkins, Lesley and Roy A. Adkins:
  Dictionary of Roman Religion New York: Facts On File, 1996

Armanino, Dominic C.:
  Dominoes: Five-Up and Other Games New York: David McKay, 1959

Bell, R. C.:
  Board and Table Games from Many Civilizations New York: Dover, 1979

Berndt, Frederick:
  The Domino Book New York: Bantam Books, 1975

Buckland, Raymond:
  Secrets of Gypsy Fortunetelling St. Paul: Llewellyn Worldwide, 1988

Buckland, Raymond:
  The Fortune-Telling Book: Encyclopedia of Divination and Soothsaying
  Detroit: Visible Ink Press, 2002

Cavendish, Marshall:
  The Book of Fate & Fortune London: Cavendish House, 1981

Cavendish, Richard:
  The Black Arts New York: G. P. Putnam's, 1967

Cheasley, Clifford W.:
  Numerology Boston: Triangle, 1916

Cheiro (Louis Hamon):
  Cheiro's Book of Numbers New York: Arc, 1964

Gibson, Walter B. & Litzka R.:
  The Complete Illustrated Book of the Psychic Sciences
  New York: Doubleday, 1966

Grady, Gary M. and Suzanne Goldberg:
  Rules of the Game: Dominoes San Francisco: Gamescape, 1995

Gypsy Queen, A:
  Zingara Fortune Teller Philadelphia: David McKay, 1901
Hargrave, Catherine Perry:
  A History of Playing Cards London: Houghton Mifflin, 1930
http://www.dominorules.com
http://www.gamecabinet.com/rules/DominoIntro.html
http://www.pagat.com/tile/wdom/
Leek, Sybil:
  Numerology: the Magic of Numbers New York: Collier, 1969
Line, Daid & Julia:
  Fortune-telling by Dice London: Aquarian Press, 1984
Lopez, Vincent:
  Numerology New York: Citadel, 1961
Müller, Reiner F.:
  Dominoes: Basic Rules and Variations New York: Sterling, 1995
Rakoczi, Basil Ivan:
  Man, Myth & Magic: Lots London: BPC Publishing, 1970
Rose, H.J.:
  Religion in Greece and Rome New York: Harper & Row, 1959
Shepard, Leslie A. (ed.):
  Encyclopedia of Occultism & Parapsychology New York: Avon 1978
Starchild, Zera:
  The Aquarian Runes Fortuna: Doorway Publications, 1993

Index

G

H

I

J

O

P

Q

R

S

T

U